CCCC
CCCCONVIVIUMPRESS
CCCC

3095

Luis F. Ladaria

Jesus Christ Salvation of All

C

CONVIVIUMPRESS

SERIES TRADITIO

2 0 0 8

Jesus Christ Salvation of All

Original Title: *Jesucristo, salvación de todos*

© SAN PABLO 2007.
© Universidad Pontificia Comillas 2007
© Luis Francisco Ladaria Ferrer 2007

Translation: *Jesus Christ Salvation of All*
© Convivium Press 2008.

http://www.conviviumpress.com
sales@conviviumpress.com
ventas@conviviumpress.com
convivium@conviviumpress.com

7661 NW 68th St, Suite 108,
Miami, Florida 33166. USA.
Phone: +1 (786) 8669718
Teléfono: +1 (786) 8798452

Edited *by* Rafael Luciani
Translated *by* María Cristina Herrera
and María Isabel Reyna
Revised *by* Miguel Arias, Doris Strieter
and Thomas Strieter
Designed *by* Eduardo Chumaceiro d'E
Series: *Traditio*

ISBN: 978-1-934996-04-1

Printed in Colombia
Impreso en Colombia
D'VINNI, S.A.

Jesus Christ Salvation of All

Contents

Introduction PAGE 9
Abbreviations PAGE 14

1

Christ: «Perfect Man» and «Man Perfected» PAGE 17

1. *The Perfection of the Humanity of Christ in Ancient Councils* PAGE 19
2. *The Perfection of the Humanity of Christ in Vatican Council II* PAGE 24
3. *Christology and Anthropology: Some Reflections* PAGE 28

2

Christian Anthropology as a Proposal for a New Humanism PAGE 37

1. *Data from Biblical Anthropology* PAGE 40
2. *Christ and Humankind in Patristic Reflections* PAGE 43
3. *Christ and Humankind in Vatican Council II and Contemporary Theological Reflection* PAGE 48
   3.1. CHRIST, PERFECT IN HUMANITY PAGE 48
   3.2. HUMANITY S DIVINE SONSHIP AS GOD'S CHILDREN PAGE 56
   3.3. CHRIST, THE MEASURE OF HUMANKIND PAGE 59
4. *A New Vision of Humanity* PAGE 63

3

Christ's Salvation and the Salvation of All PAGE 65

1. *Salvation: God, Humanity and Encounter* PAGE 67
2. *Salvation in Christ* PAGE 74
3. *Christ's «Perfection»: Origin of Our Salvation* PAGE 76
4. *God's Son in Union with Every Human Being* PAGE 84
5. *Eschatological Perspectives* PAGE 90
6. *Offering Salvation* PAGE 95

4

God's Incarnation and Christian Theology of Religions PAGE 97

1. *The Incarnation: A Unique and Non-Repeatable Event* PAGE 100
2. *«The Son of God Is Somehow in Union with Every Human Being»* PAGE 103
3. *The Incarnation and Definition of Humanity* PAGE 106
4. *The Universal Relevance of the Incarnation and the Theology of Religions* PAGE 108
5. *The Incarnation and the Gift of the Spirit* PAGE 114
6. *The Configuration with the Glorified Christ: Fullness for All Humanity* PAGE 117
7. *Open reflections: the Universal Presence of the Spirit of Christ* PAGE 118

5

Christianity and the Universality of Salvation PAGE 121

1. *Guidelines from the Second Vatican Council* PAGE 123
2. *Developments in Recent Theology on the Universality of Salvation* PAGE 126
3. *The Universality of Salvation and Christ's Unique Mediation* PAGE 132
4. *The Universality of the Gift of the Spirit* PAGE 145
5. *The Symphony of Salvation* PAGE 148

Introduction

In today's debate on the uniqueness and universality of the saving action of Jesus Christ, I have been repeatedly asked to touch upon the theme of salvation. Why is Christ the Savior of all? Why should we Christians maintain this position which is often considered unintelligible and even scandalous to many of our fellow human beings? In fact, as we begin to reflect on soteriology and Christian anthropology, we gain the awareness that the very nature of salvation —as presented in the New Testament and in the teachings of the Church— is that it is the vocation and ultimate perfection of all human beings, which cannot be explained without Christ. By his death and resurrection, he has conquered sin and death and has given us his very life in such a manner that the salvation he offers us cannot be separated from his very person.

The title of this book proposes Jesus Christ as *salvation for all* humanity and not merely as its *Savior*. To make this explicit, from the beginning, this intimate relationship which Jesus has brought us is not simply a gift that is separate from his person, as great as the gift may be. Indeed, upon coming into the world, he brings us all the good news within himself (Saint Irenaeus of Lyons). Jesus, with all his human history, especially his death and resurrection, makes us part and parcel of his very life, which he as a human being attained in fullness at his resurrection when he was glorified by the Father. The resurrection and glorification of Christ, which become the perfection of the human nature that he assumed, are the foundation of our own fulfillment. Because he has died and risen, we too may walk with him from death to life.

Human salvation and fullness mean participation in the glory of Christ, which he possesses in the humanity he assumed at the incarnation and which he has never abandoned nor of which he will ever be stripped . For all eternity, God's Son exists as God and as man, as eternal Son of the Father and as head of humanity.

The tradition of the Church has often spoken about the intimate union between Christ and all of humanity. The Second Vatican Council (cfr. GS 22) has echoed this teaching by affirming that the Son of God, through his incarnation, has somehow become one with every human being. This assumption makes it unthinkable that the divine life of Christ as head would not also be that of his whole body. The communication of new life by the risen Lord and the Son's union with all of humanity through his incarnation are two inseparable faces of the same coin. In his infinite benevolence, God's only Son wanted to be the firstborn among many (cfr. Rom 8:29). Thus, he irrevocably associated our destiny with his own. In him, as a gift of the Holy Spirit who makes us one body, humanity acquires the most solid and definitive union. We cannot separate Christ from his Church, which is his body, but neither can we separate him from the human race in its totality, as the Lord has united himself with all of us, and he died and rose for all of us. Christ is Savior of all humanity because, as the incarnate Son, he is the only one who can bring all of humanity to the Father (cfr. John 14:6). The path and its final destination cannot be torn asunder. Only the Son, in the power of his Spirit, can make us fully children of God. Only in union with him, the «perfect man» (cfr. GS 22, 41), do we attain fullness. On the other hand, Jesus will take us to the Father, from whom he himself has come, whom he called upon during his earthly life, and to whom he returned after fulfilling the task the very same Father had entrusted to him. Jesus the Son makes us children of God in himself. Only in this way do we participate in the life of the one and triune God —Father, Son and Holy Spirit. This is the sole divine vocation of all humanity.

Through paths known only to God, the Holy Spirit provides all of us with the possibility of being part of the paschal mystery (cfr. GS 22). We Christians have become part of this mystery of death and resurrection through our baptism. No human being may remain indifferent about this incorporation into Christ and his Church. The saving influence of Jesus and his Spirit know no bounds: Christ's mediation is universal. Also, the role of Jesus as the sole mediator cannot ever be considered as a stage in a process which must be surmounted. Only in union with him do we receive the first fruits of God's life, and only in him will we fully experience the eschatological consummation. Salvation in Christ is possible for all humanity, and on the horizon of theological reflection the hope may arise that this salvation will indeed reach everyone. But salvation itself would become denaturalized if its absolute certainty would be affirmed and if we lost sight of the possibility of damnation. God offers us his fullness in a limitless act of love that can only be accepted in love itself. Our free response to divine love is an essential dimension of Christian salvation. Thus, the awesome possibility of saying no to God remains open to every human being.

The fundamental anthropological issue of humanity's relationship with Christ, beginning with creation, is intimately linked to the question of salvation in Christ. Christ, the image of the invisible God, is the model of humanity. God shaped the first Adam with features that were eventually assumed by the second Adam. With forthcoming distinctions still to be made, the fact remains that by the very act of creation, with the whole of creation being realized in Christ and through Christ, no one will remain beyond Christ's reach and not be touched by his light (cfr. John 1:9).

If salvation, which is an undeserved gift, is not something extrinsic to humanity, then Christ cannot be seen merely as the final word on the subject, but the first word as well. Salvation, in all its unforeseen newness, must bring humanity to its intrinsic fulfillment. Christ's presence in the very definition of humanity and the initial human vocation to conform ourselves to him are in direct relationship with Christ's unique and universal mediation. It is no wonder the New Testament invites us to embrace his creative mediation and salvation (cfr. Col 1:15-20). Both of them imply the other. He, who is the origin of all that we are, saves us and brings us to fulfillment. At the same time, our origin in Christ has its sight forever set on the perfection of the Risen One. The doctrine of the divine image and likeness originating in Christ, as the image of the invisible God (cfr. Col 1:15; 2 Cor 4:4), undoubtedly has many points in common with the universality of Christ's saving mediation. The Church's teaching and theology of the last several decades have at various times addressed the «protological» relevance of Christology, which was so decisive in the patristic era, but had been in part forgotten over the centuries. The incarnation, death, and resurrection of Jesus form the core of the divine plan. Thus, the creation of the world and of humanity is to be understood in light of this core. At the same time, it is from this core that the renewing gift of the Spirit flows, which is the jewel of eternal life and the first fruits of our eschatological fullness.

The universal mediation of Jesus and the significance of Christology for the doctrine of the creation of humanity are the main themes which, from diverse viewpoints and with some variation, are addressed in this volume. We have approached identical or similar themes from various perspectives, to give a broad approach to the delicate theme contents treated here. The data and citations used throughout the various cchapters, have distinct functions in different contexts. It is often very useful to repeat develop theological the same ideas and realities from a variety of angles and points of view. It is hoped that this new volume will be a contribution to this relevant debate in contemporary theology.

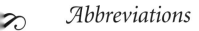 *Abbreviations*

CCL

Corpus Christianorum Series Latina (Turnhout, Belgium)

❧

CSEL

Corpus Scriptorum Ecclesiasticorum Latinorum (Wien, Austria)

❧

DH

Denzinger-Hünermann, *Enchiridion Symbolorum. Definitionum et declarationum de rebus fidei et morum* (Freiburg, Germany)

❧

DV

Dei Verbum (Second Vatican Council: *Dogmatic Constitution on Divine Revelation*)

❧

FP

Fuentes Patrísticas (Madrid, Spain)

❧

GS

Gaudium et Spes (Second Vatican Council: *Pastoral Constitution on the Church in the Modern World*)

❧

PLS

Patrologia Latina Suplementum (Paris, France)

❧

SCh

Sources Chrétiennes (Paris, France)

❧

TS

Patristische Texte und Studien (Berlin, Germany)

❧

Christ: «Perfect Man» and «Man Perfected»

1

The Perfection of the Humanity of Christ in Ancient Councils

The Christological dogma of the Church, with its deep roots in the New Testament, has affirmed the fullness of the humanity of Jesus[1], not as an abstraction but in complete solidarity with us. The Council of Chalcedon maintains in its well-known text that «one and the same Son, our Lord Jesus Christ: the same perfect in divinity and perfect in humanity, the same truly God and truly man…; consubstantial with the Father in regard to his divinity, and the same consubstantial with us in regard to his humanity; like us in all respects except for sin (cfr. Heb 4:15); begotten before the ages from the Father in regard to his divinity, and in the last days the same for us and for our salvation from Mary, the virgin God-bearer in regard to his humanity»[2]. The point of reference is not only the perfection of humanity by the Son's assumption of all humanity, namely, a body and a rational soul[3], but his consubstantiality «with us», with real, concrete people whose condition he fully shares with the exception of sin[4]. In any case, it is evident that, in the approximation to the mystery of Christ's humanity, the immediate point of reference is our specific condition. The New Testament overall presupposes it, and in some passages the idea is affirmed with special clarity (Gal 4:4: «born of a woman, born under the law»; Rom 8:3: God did «by sending his own Son in the likeness of sinful flesh»). Jesus saves us by sharing the reality of our life. Not only human nature in abstract, but our real situation; from it Jesus saves us in concrete terms by carrying upon himself our sin, he who has not known sin (cfr. 2 Cor 5:21; Gal 3:13; 1 Pet 2:21-22). This last aspect, as we shall see, gains special significance.

---

1 Cfr. LADARIA L.F., «Cristo "perfecto hombre" y "hombre perfecto"» in BENAVENT V.E. - MORALI I. (eds.), *Sentire cum Ecclesia. Homenaje al P. Karl Josef Backer, SJ*, Valencia-Roma 2003, 171-185.

2 DH 301. As it is known, a large part of this text and, in fact, the dual consubstantiality with the Father and with us finds its root in the so-called «union formula» between Cyril of Alexandria and bishops from the Church of Antioch in 433 (DH 271-273).

3 GREGORY OF NAZIANZUS, *Ep.* 101 I 32 (SCh 208,50): «That which has not been assumed has not been redeemed; that which has joined God is saved», a classic formulation of a principle repeated in varied ways. The underscoring of the integrity of the human nature in Jesus shows an evident soteriological concern.

4 The Council refers to Heb 4:15, although it is not a direct quote, it says «in everything like us except for sin». Hebrews says «tested in everything like us except for sin».

The statement of the perfection of the humanity of Christ presumes that we know, at least initially, what it means to be a man. It also presupposes the conviction that sin is not part of that perfection, but that it is the main assault against it. The fact that we are told that the Son has assumed «human nature» expresses all of the «realism of solidarity»[5], which he demonstrates by sharing our condition in order to free us from sin and communicate divine life. The perfection of the humanity proclaimed about Christ, to begin with, means he is a complete man and not just in part, namely, the fact that he has assumed a rational body and soul, acquires implicitly, in the same formula, a fuller and more radical meaning. The humanity of Jesus is not simply complete in the sense that there is nothing missing—against any Apollinarist or Monophysite reduction, but at the same time, although in an implicit manner, a perfection is suggested that consists in a growth of humanity parallel to the deprivation and *kenosis* of the Son of God[6]. Later evolution will contribute further to identify the contents and scope of the perfection of humanity in Christ, which is free of the stain of sin that affects all of humanity.

This will in fact occur at the Second and Third Councils of Constantinople. In the Second Council (553), it will be clarified that the unity of subject in Christ, namely, that his sole person is that of the divine Word, does not mean that the assumed humanity has no relevance for the person of the Word. The hypostatic union is interpreted as a union «according to composition»[7] in such a way that it may be said that, after the incarnation the sole person of the Son becomes a «composite person»[8]. The subject of all actions, the Word, does not act without the presence of the human nature that he has appropriated, which he has made his own in a definite way[9]. After the incarnation, the person of the Word exists only in this «composition» with human nature assumed for our salvation. And this nature is now whole and perfected because it is the human nature of the Son.

---

5 BORDONI M., *Gesù di Nazaret Signore e Cristo 3. Il Cristo annunziato dalla Chiesa*, Roma 1986, 844.

6 LEO THE GREAT, *Tomus ad Flavianum* (DH 293): «Adsumpsit formam servi sine sorde peccati, humana augens, divina non minuens». The idea of the elevation of humanity by the incarnation of the Son is thus present in the historical context of Chalcedon.

7 DH 424-425: «… the union of the Word of God with the animated flesh of a rational and intelligent soul was made by composition or by hypostasis, according to the holy fathers … The Holy Church of God, rejecting the impiety of one or the other heresy (of Apollinaris and Eutyches), proclaims the union of the Word of God with flesh by composition, that is, by hypostasis, because union by composition in the mystery of Christ does not only keep without confusion the elements that join but also does not admit division». The language of the Council of Chalcedon is evident.

8 Cfr. THOMAS AQUINAS, *STh.* III 2,4.

9 POPE SAINT LEO THE GREAT, before and after Chalcedon: cfr. DH 294; 318.

The Third Council of Constantinople (680-681) insisted with even greater clarity on the perfection of the Son's human nature, in this case with a clear overall soteriological concern. Indeed, with the insistence on the perfection of humanity, which includes human free will[10], it goes deeper, and in a new way, into what the absence of sin in Christ means: the Son's will is identical to that of the Father, in keeping with the known principle of the existence of one will in the Holy Trinity[11]. At the same time, in his human will, which is different from the divine will, but in perfect submission to it at every moment, Jesus obeys the Father; hence, the formula of Chalcedon «except sin» gains all of its meaning and the perfection of the humanity of Christ with all of its relevance: «The humanity of Jesus is the incarnate expression, the temporal shaping of his eternal Sonship. That is why it has all the fullness that finitude, individuality and temporality allow. However, as the humanity of God, it is the most thoroughly human and its freedom the most perfect which can rule over itself and before God, and thus it is without sin»[12]. The human volition of Jesus, while it underscores the perfection of his humanity, shows the depth of his condition as Son in perfect submission to the Father. The completion of God's purpose is the perfection of the creature, which exists and is able to exist only in reference to the Creator. The freedom of Christ as a man, insofar as it is sustained by the person of the Son, is the fullest that one could conceive; it is more complete than could even be imagined. On the one hand, the human volition of Jesus is totally guided by that of the Son, and on the other hand, the Son expresses himself and assumes the human will of Christ as his own. Also, as a man, Christ freely delivers himself to the Father, thus bringing about our salvation. In this way, he can intercede on our behalf (cfr. Rom 8:34; Heb 7:23; 9:24; 1 John 2:1) and take our place before the Father. There is only one mediator between God and humanity, the man Christ Jesus (cfr. 1 Tim 2:5).

The perfection of the humanity of Christ, his solidarity with us, his absence of sin, and the existence of his human volition in perfect submission to divine

10 DH 556: «And we proclaim equally two natural volitions or wills in him and two natural principles of action … And the two natural wills not in opposition … but his human will following, and not resisting or struggling, rather in fact subject to his divine and all powerful will … For just as his flesh is said to be and is flesh of the Word of God, so too the natural will of his flesh is said to and does belong to the Word of God … For in the same way that his all holy and blameless animate flesh was not destroyed in being made divine but remained in its own limit and category, so his human will as well was not destroyed by being made divine».

11 Cfr. DH 172; 501; 542; 544; 545; 546; 572; 680; 851.

12 GONZÁLEZ DE CARDEDAL O., *Cristología*, Madrid 2001, 269.

will are all necessarily related. Humanity is perfect insofar as it is complete, but more so because Jesus, not having sinned as a man, can fully deliver himself to the Father on our behalf. Ultimately, this is true because the creature does not disappear or diminish by closer proximity to the Creator; rather, because of this, the creature gains greater perfection. If the hypostatic union is the greatest union between God and humanity, then in Jesus —and in no other— should the perfection of humanity be sought, not in spite of, but because of his divinity[13]. Thus, «we must conceive the relationship of the person of the Logos with his human nature in such a way that, in it, autonomy and radical nearness may reach the supreme, unique degree, qualitatively non-measurable with other cases, although always within the creator-creature setting»[14]. These reflections took place, as is well known, in a study about the Council of Chalcedon. This Council limited itself to point out explicitly that the humanity of Christ is complete, as the Council of Ephesus had already done. The later dogmatic developments of the ancient Church, however, help to show clearly how the dynamics of the Fourth Ecumenical Council contain the seeds of truths that were later developed. In fact, the explicit mention of the absence of sin points to something more than humanity complete in itself. The Christological dogma has further reflected on the impeccability of Christ, on his perfect freedom, and on his full response to God as a man, by virtue of which he may free us from our disobedience and sin. Jesus had not only *not* sinned, but in fact *could* not sin because of his condition as Son, that is, his being in complete relationship with the Father. He did not become blameless by virtue of his moral efforts[15]. In not being able to sin, the perfection of freedom is found, not its limitation[16]. And even if Jesus does not have a human freedom different from the divine one, this does not mean that this freedom is not genuinely human: the freedom of the Son is exercised in the proper mode of human freedom, both in time and history[17]. The perfection

13 It is necessary to mention the well-known article by RAHNER K., «Problemas actuales de Cristología» in *Escritos de Teología* I, Madrid 1963, 169-222, which has had great influence on Christological studies in recent years. Rahner voices the fundamental thesis on p. 183 (of the Spanish edition cited): «the radical dependence on God does not grow in inverse ratio, but in a direct one with true autonomy vis-à-vis Him».

14 RAHNER K., «Problemas actuales de Cristología» in *Escritos de Teología* I, 183; and cfr. also p. 185: «the movement of creation would appear looming beforehand towards that point in which God reaches simultaneously supreme nearness and remoteness in face of that which is different from him —what is created».

15 Cfr. DH 434.

16 Cfr. GONZÁLEZ DE CARDEDAL O., *Cristología*, Madrid 2001, 477, citing THOMAS AQUINAS, *STh.* I 62,8.

17 KASPER W., *Jesús el Cristo*, Salamanca 1978, 292: «Only God may be thought of in such a "supraessential" and "sovereign and free" mode, that makes free in its most intimate uniqueness what is

of his human nature is not reduced to the fact of its being complete. We must keep in mind in this context the fact that in his life of perfect obedience as Son of the Father, fulfilled in his passion and death, Jesus has reached «perfection», thanks to the fact that he is the cause of eternal salvation for all those who obey him (cfr. Heb 5:8-9).

Evidently, we cannot think of the incarnation of the Son except from the basis of our human condition fully shared by him, but undoubtedly Christian thought has suggested perspectives beyond this point of reflection. That was the experience of those encountering Jesus during their own mortal lives (cfr. Mark 1:22-27; 2:12; 7:37; 12:17). To follow him in his concrete way of living is to find life. Saint Paul has spoken of Christ as the last and second Adam (cfr. 1 Cor 15:45-47), that is, the definitive image of humanity; in Christ, both Jews and Gentiles become one «new man» (cfr. Eph 2:15). Thus, Christ becomes the prototype of humanity, whom he has saved and redeemed. He has shared our condition and saved us; through his dying and rising from the dead, he has made us participants in his life. It is thus inevitable to conclude that, since he was a man as we are, then, having fulfilled the will of his Father during his earthly life through his death and resurrection, it seems clear that humanity's destiny is to become like Christ. If, at first, the human condition is the point of reference needed to understand the meaning of the incarnation of the Son of God, moving therefore from Adam to Christ, one discovers that Jesus is the model that humanity should follow; but then the pattern moves from Christ to Adam, «who was a type of the one who was to come» (Rom 5:14)[18]. The ancient councils did not develop these ideas, among other reasons, because they did not make explicit the problems concerning the constitution of Christ and the underlying soteriological issue. But on the eve of the Council of Chalcedon, Saint Leo the Great indicated that the Son of God, by assuming the form of a servant, elevated the human *(humana augens)*

---

distinct from himself, precisely when uniting it to himself totally». Cfr. BORDONI M., *Gesù di Nazaret. Signore e Cristo. 3. Il Cristo annunziato dalla Chiesa*, Roma 1986, 856. SESBOÜÉ B., *Jésus-Christ dans la tradition de l'Église*, Paris 1982, 177, on the distinction between will and freedom. The former takes the side of nature and thus one must speak of two wills. The latter takes the side of the person; thus, freedom is singular. One cannot speak of the human person apart from the divine one; hence, neither can one speak about freedom. But divine freedom has become human in Jesus, who has placed his own personal freedom in a human nature and has exercised it humanly.

18 Although it must be kept in mind that in this context Paul refers, above all, to the redemption and liberation from sin that weighs on all as a consequence of Adam's sin, it does not directly consider humanity's conformity with Christ.

without diminishing the divine[19]. In this way, an indirect understanding that human nature attains in Jesus a new and unique perfection is achieved[20]. The absence of sin in Jesus does not seem foreign to the excellence of his humanity[21].

2
The Perfection of the Humanity of Christ in Vatican Council II

The perfection of the humanity of Christ that was underscored by the ancient councils was further developed in the context of the ancient writers, who expressed that it was not only the complete character of human nature that was at stake, but also the paradigmatic character of the humanity of Jesus, which is a consequence of the dignity that comes with him being the Son and the moral perfection that accompanies it. In this sense we can perceive a profound continuity, even with the difference that undoubtedly appears between the ancient definitions and the Second Vatican Council, which has explicitly spoken of Christ not only as a perfect man, but also as man perfected:

> Christ, the final Adam, by the revelation of the mystery of the Father and his love, fully reveals man to man himself and makes his supreme calling clear... He who is «the image of the invisible God» (Col 1:15), is himself the perfect man (*homo perfectus*). To the sons of Adam he restores the divine likeness which had been disfigured from the first sin onward. Since human nature as he assumed it was not annulled, by that very fact it has been raised up to a divine dignity in our respect too. For by his incarnation the Son of God has united himself in some fashion with every man (GS 22).

We will not enter into a detailed analysis of this text here[22]. We will simply highlight some aspects of interest to our purpose. First and foremost, it is clear

---

19 Cfr. LEO THE GREAT, *Tomus ad Flavianum* (DH 293).
20 Cfr. also LEO THE GREAT from the letter *Licet per nostros* (DH 297); «nec damnum sui recipiens nec augmentum et sic adsumptam naturam beatificans, ut glorificata in glorificante permaneat».
21 Ibid., (DH 299): «Nec alio illi quam ceteris hominibus anima est inspirata principio, quae excelleret non diversitate generis sed sublimitate virtutis».
22 Cfr. LADARIA L.F., «El hombre a la luz de Cristo en el concilio Vaticano II» in LATOURELLE R., (ed.), *Vaticano II: balance y perspectivas*, Salamanca 1989, 705-714; GERTLER T., *Jesus Christus. Die Antwort der Kirche auf die Frage nach dem Menschsein. Eine Untersuchung zu Funktion und Inhalt der Christologie im ersten Teil der Pastoralkonstitution «Gaudium et Spes» des Zweiten Vatikanischen Konzil*, Leipzig 1986.

that Vatican II takes a different perspective from that of the old ecclesial documents. Indeed, some knowledge about humanity is assumed before taking on the study of Christ as the «new man», as the «*novissimus Adam*», which is the heading of this paragraph of the pastoral constitution. But the second part of the process is made explicit. Once Christ and his life are known, it is clear that «the mystery of man is only clarified in the mystery of the Incarnate Word. Adam, the first man, was the figure of him that was to come»[23]. Therefore, it seems to suggest that the perfection of the humanity of Jesus is not only placed in an eschatological sphere, but also in a protological one: he is the model and Paradigm in whom we human beings reach fullness, because from the start he is the model in whose image humanity has been created. If the first part of this affirmation has always been present in the consciousness of the Church, this cannot be said about the second, well-documented one, the general thinking of the first few centuries of the Christian era notwithstanding. Christ, who became incarnate, has been the model and Paradigm for humanity from the beginning, ever since we were molded from the virgin soil of the earthly paradise[24].

23 *Gaudium et Spes* 22. These words are the beginning of this volume. The text refers to Rom 5:14, which we have cited before. We noted that these Pauline words are in the context that speaks about the liberation from sin. But the Council seems to use it in a broader sense, as can also be inferred from TERTULLIAN's quote *De carnis resurrectione (De resurrectione mortuorum)* 6: «Quodcumque enim limus exprimebatur, Christus cogitabatur homo futurus».

24 The text of TERTULLIAN cited in *Gaudium et Spes* 22, to which we have just referred, continues as follows (CCL 2,928): «Id utique quod finxit, ad imaginem Dei fecit illum scilicet Christi… Ita limus ille, iam tunc imaginem induens Christi futuri in carne, non tantum Dei opus erat, sed et pignus». Cfr. *Adv. Prax.* XII 3-4 (CCL 2,1173): «Cum quibus enim faciebat hominem et quibus faciebat similem, Filio quidem qui erat induiturus hominem, Spiritui veto qui erat sanctificaturus hominem… Erat autem ad cuius imaginem facebat, ad Filii scilicet, qui homo futurus certior et verior, imaginem suam dici hominem qui tunc de limo formari habebat, imago veri et similitudo». Cfr. *Adv. Marc.* V 8,1 (CCL 1,685). IRENAEUS OF LYONS, *Demonstr.* 22 (FP 2,106): «and the image of God is the Son in whose image man has been made. This is why in latter times it has manifested itself to make it understood that the image was alike to himself»; *Demonstr.* 32 (123): «hence, from this earth still virgin, God took mud and made man, foundation of the human race. Thus, to fulfill this man, the Lord assumed the same bodily disposition, was born of a Virgin by the will and wisdom of God, in order to also manifest the identity of his bodily composition with that of Adam and for the fulfillment of what had been written at the beginning: man in the image and likeness of God». Cfr. also IRENAEUS OF LYONS, *Adv. Haer.* III 21,10; 22,3 (SCh 211, 428-430; 438); V 16,2 (SCh 153, 216). This Christological idea of the *imago*, although coexisting with other ideas, was kept alive in the West still during the IV and V Centuries. Cfr. HILARY OF POITIERS, *Myst.* I 2 (SCh 18,76); PETER CHRYSOLOGUS, *Ser.* 117,1-2 (CCL, 24A, 709); GREGORY OF ELVIRA, *Trac. Orig.* XIV 25 (FP 9, 344); XVI 22 (374); AURELIUS PRUDENTIUS, *Apotheosis* v. 309 and 1040 (*Obras Completas*, BAC, Madrid 1981, 200; 240). References on the theme in Eastern theology will be found in GROSSI v., *Lineamenta di antropologia patristica*, Roma 1983, 61-62. Cfr. for this theme: LADARIA L.F., «El hombre creado a imagen de Dios» in SESBOÜÉ B. (ed.), *El hombre y su salvación* (Historia de los Dogmas 2), Salamanca 1996, 75-115, esp. 78-82.

From this idea, which we find merely suggested in Vatican II, the «perfection» of the humanity of Jesus, as well as the anthropological consequences that this entails, gains very clear connotations. Christ is the model after which humanity was created. This fact cannot be separated from the human vocation to conform itself to Christ; rather, it constitutes its premise[25]; the reproduction of the image of Christ may be the intrinsic perfection of humanity because it has been God's intention for us, since the beginning of time, to attain the perfect likeness of his Son. There is no other ultimate vocation for human beings, if it is not God himself[26]. Because of this, following Christ is tantamount to perfection since he is the very being of humanity itself, as indicated by Vatican II[27]. The sole divine vocation for humanity thus gains a clear Christological connotation.

Human nature has been assumed, not absorbed in Christ. The teaching of Vatican II depends on numerous texts belonging to the tradition to which we have already made reference[28]. But the conciliar pronouncement goes even further. Christ's human nature has been neither annulled nor absorbed by his divinity; rather, it has been elevated to a sublime dignity «also in us». The text presupposes that this sublime dignity primarily corresponds to the humanity of Jesus. But between Jesus and us there is an intrinsic relationship. The hypostatic union is a unique and unrepeatable fact, but the Son of God, through his incarnation, has joined «in a certain way [*quodammodo*] every man». The so-called vagueness of this formulation does not mean that the deep reality that it expresses is minimized[29]; it simply wishes to stress the difference with the hypostatic union, which is unique and unrepeatable.

---

25 *Gaudium et Spes* 22, after the passage we have cited in the text: «The Christian man, conformed to the likeness of that Son who is the firstborn within a large family, (cfr. Rom 8:29; Col 1:18) received "the first-fruits of the Spirit" (Rom 8:23) by which he becomes capable of discharging the new law of love... linked with the paschal mystery and patterned on the dying Christ, he will hasten forward to resurrection in the strength which comes from hope. All this holds true not only for Christians, but for all men of good will in whose hearts grace works in an unseen way. For, since Christ died for all men, and since the ultimate vocation of man is in fact one and divine, we ought to believe that the Holy Spirit in a manner known only to God offers to every man the possibility of being associated with this paschal mystery».

26 *Gaudium et Spes* 24: «All... men are called to one and the same goal, namely God Himself»; cfr. also *Gaudium et Spes* 22, text cited in the previous note.

27 *Gaudium et Spes* 22: «He who follows Christ, perfect man (*homo perfectus*) makes himself more of a man». In other places of DS the traditional formula of *perfectus homo* is used; cfr. *Gaudium et Spes* 38; 45.

28 In fact, the Councils of Constantinople II and III and the Council of Chalcedon are cited: cfr. nos. 3 and 4 in *Gaudium et Spes* 22.

29 This is not the place to deal with this problem about the inclusion of the humanity in Christ. Besides *Gaudium et Spes* 22, comments on the union of all people in Christ are found in nos. 24

The elevation of human nature, which takes place by the fact that the Son has assumed it, has consequences for all of humanity. This is another dimension of the perfection of the humanity of Christ that has undoubted soteriological repercussions. Even if not always made explicit, the soteriological dimension is always present in the Christological dogma. If in the early centuries of the Church the integrity of the human nature of Jesus guaranteed salvation for the whole man in all dimensions, the perfection of the humanity of Jesus, with the dimensions that now stand in relief, shows us that in the configuration with Christ, which he himself makes possible by sharing our condition, lies man's perfection. Humanity is enhanced by its being assumed by the Son of God. The expression of Saint Leo the Great, *humana augens,* seems to resound in Vatican II with a more explicit reference to all people[30]. If the first movement goes from Adam to Christ, to understand who Christ is, then very quickly, in light of the faith, the opposite step becomes necessary to understand the depth of the human being. Saint Ignatius of Antioch believed that he would become a man through martyrdom, which would conform him with Christ, and thus attain the pure light of God[31]. From Adam to Christ and from Christ to Adam are two interrelated movements, each of them bound mutually to the other. If initially the former prevails, then afterward it is the latter that, without erasing the former, gains primacy. Hans Urs von Balthasar has piercingly pointed to this reciprocal priority of Christ and Adam: «in Christ God and man reflect each other in the infinite, because in a sense he is the result of the encounter of both natures, but in another sense, he himself as divine person determines the relationship and the distance between God and man. As Redeemer he is after sin, but as image and head of creation he is before it»[32].

and 32. The theme has been abundantly developed in the patristic era, also in terms of the theme of the Church as the Body of Christ. A succinct treatment of the subject with enough information will be found in GONZÁLEZ DE CARDEDAL O., *Cristología,* BAC, Madrid 2001, 525-528.

30 Cfr. nos. 6 and 19 of *Gaudium et Spes* 22. COMISIÓN TOLÓGICA INTERNACIONAL, *Documentos 1969-1996,* POZO C., S.J. (ed.) BAC, Madrid 1998, I E) 4, Madrid 1998, 254: «The more profoundly Jesus Christ participates in human misery, the higher humans climb in participation with divine life». Available in English: International Theological Commission: *Texts and Documents (1969-1985),* Ignatius Press, San Francisco 1989.

31 *To the Romans,* VI 2-3 (FP 1,157): «Let me reach pure light. When it happens, I will be a man. Allow me to imitate the passion of my God».

32 VON BALTHASAR H.U., *Das Weizenkorn. Aphorismus,* Einsiedeln 1989³, 60, cited in CORDOVILLA A., *Gramática de la encarnación. La creación en Cristo en la teología de K. Rahner y Hans Urs von Balthasar,* Madrid 2004, 243. Also cfr. VON BALTHASAR H.U., *Teodramática 4. La acción,* Madrid 1995, 448: «The First Adam, by himself, is not able to reach completion; what he has to do is die to himself to be raised and integrated into the second one. For this to be possible it is due to the Second Adam, who being his end is also his beginning».

3

Christology and Anthropology: Some Reflections

Christ is the first model of creation. In his image humanity has been created. In him we were predestined before the creation of the world (cfr. Eph 1:3-10). We are called to conform ourselves to him, and there is no human destiny other than this one (cfr. Rom 8:29; 1 Cor 15:49). If Christ is the perfection of the human person, salvation in him is the sole fullness of humanity. God has created us with him in mind, and in this sense he must be given the primacy of everything. Starting with *homo perfectus,* we may come to understand what we are. The mystery of humanity only becomes clear in the mystery of the incarnate Word. When God was molding the first Adam (*primus homo*), he had the second in mind (*novissimus Adam*). In this sense we have a clear movement from Christ to Adam. But at the same time we should keep in mind the chronological priority of the first Adam and the fact that it is impossible, due to our condition, to become the perfect man without God's direct intervention in the incarnation of his Son, the model and Paradigm of humanity. We stand before a radical newness. We can contemplate with our own eyes the perfection of humanity only because Jesus came to share in our condition fully, sent by God «in the likeness of sinful flesh» (cfr. Rom 8:3). Thanks to his sharing in our condition, he was able to rescue us from it. In the concrete way in which the Son of God appeared on earth, human sin has its role. The obedience of Christ has had to inversely follow the steps of Adam's disobedience. The path from the first Adam to the second is not only placed under the sign of continuity but also under the sign of rupture. This is demonstrated by the mystery of the cross of Christ, from which the new life of humanity has flowed. Both aspects have to be taken into account at the same time, in order to do justice to the New Testament and the tradition of the Church. We will now attempt a brief synthesis of these diverse aspects.

1) First and foremost, it is necessary to insist on the unity of God's design that embraces creation and humanity's salvation through the Son's incarnation. Creation in Christ —and not solely in the Son— is a fundamental truth of Christianity reevaluated by recent theology. There will be no need to give much reflection to Karl Rahner's considerations about the possibility of the incarnation as a condition for the possibility of creation. And this is so because what sustains the possibility of God expressing himself in creation is the divine pos-

sibility of creating by assuming and making complete his creative reality. This, and in particular the creation of man, constitutes the «grammar» of his revelation and full self-expression in the incarnation of the Son[33].

In reality, the awareness of the consummation of everything in Christ necessarily makes us consider the problem of the creation of everything in him, that is, if we do not want salvation to come to all people apart from Christ. It is what would inevitably occur if the eschatological consummation in Christ would not be accompanied by a corresponding protology:

> As a last consequence emerges the mediating function in creation, not only of the Logos, but of Christ. This means that all things have been made only in reference to their consummation in the second Adam, which is only perceptible in the being and knowledge of the Son who brings to consummation his task. Once more, none other than the Creator could have given this role to him, as the actor of the consummation; otherwise he could not have carried it out *from within*. Rather, he would have had to stamp his final mark *from without* on things created with a different origin than his own[34].

---

33 Cfr. RAHNER K., «Para la teología de la encarnación» in *Escritos de Teología* IV, Madrid 1964, 139-157, esp. 151-152; human being is what emerges when God wants to be no-god. Also ibid., 153; RAHNER K., *Grundkurs des Glaubens,* Friburgo-Basilea-Viena 1976, 220-225. Also VON BALTHASAR H.U. mentions the grammar of creation in *Theologik II. Wahrheit Gottes,* Einsiedeln 1985, 73: «The natural human being knows what ethics and practical reason is, and people of the Old Testament also know what should be the just relationship with the living God. Into this grammar, Jesus can stamp God's word». Ibid., 76: «God has made the creature in his image and likeness so that he, through his grace, may be capable, from within, to serve as a sounding board by which God can express himself and be understood»; «…divine logic wishes and is able to express itself in human logic, due to an *analogia linguae* and finally —in spite all objections— also *entis,* as this perfects itself in Christ, God and humankind in one Person».

34 VON BALTHASAR H.U., *Teodramática 3. Las personas del drama: el hombre en Cristo,* Madrid 1993, 237-238. Cfr. also *Zu seinem Werk,* Einsiedeln 2000, 24; the «towards Christ» of creation requires a corresponding protology. PANNENBERG W., *Systematic Theology* II, Madrid 1996, 25: «the affirmation of the mediation of the Son in creation must be understood here [Heb 1:1; Col 1:16,20; Eph 1:10], to begin with, in a *final* sense. It means that only in Jesus Christ will the creation of the world be consummated. But as correct as this viewpoint may be … the creative mediation of the Son cannot be limited to this aspect. The final ordering of creatures to the manifestation of Jesus Christ rather supposes that creatures have the origin of their being and existence in the Son. Otherwise, the final recapitulation of all things in the Son (Eph 1:10) would be outside things themselves, and this would suppose that it would not be the definitive consummation of the authentic being of created realities». PANNENBERG applies this idea specifically to humankind in *Systematic Theology* II, 245-247: «the intention of the *Creator* cannot be placed in such an extrinsic and inefficient fashion in relation to his creature».

What is said here in general terms about creation finds a special application to humanity. Anthropology only reaches its full form in Christology; for this reason, it should be shaped by it from the beginning[35]. The first Adam derives his meaning from the second. For Christians, only in view of Christ do we get the true sense of the human being. We cannot presuppose a complete idea of man and his destiny prior to Jesus.

2) This unity of the divine design embracing creation and incarnation, based on which we must say that the second is the ultimate sense of the first, cannot make us forget the radical newness of the Christ event. We have already encountered this idea. Christ absolutely cannot be deduced from man, who is created in his image and called to be like him and to conform to him. This newness is indicated in different aspects:

a) First, this newness means that only in Christ is God's design, hidden since the creation of the world, revealed: «This mystery was not made known to humankind as it has now been revealed to his holy apostles and prophets by the Spirit... Although I am the very least of all the saints, this grace was given me to bring to the Gentiles the news of the boundless riches of Christ, and to make everyone see what is the plan of the mystery hidden for ages in God, who created all things» (Eph 3:4-5, together with Eph 3:8-9). And also: «Now to God who is able to strengthen you according to my gospel and the proclamation of Jesus Christ, according to the revelation of the mystery that was kept secret for long ages, but is now disclosed and through the prophetic writings is made known...» (Rom 16:25-26); «... to fulfill God's word, the mystery hidden for centuries and generations and now manifested to his saints»[36]. The singleness of the divine design is perfectly compatible with progress in its revelation. What God had projected for all time in Christ has not been revealed until his appearance.

---

35 VON BALTHASAR H.U., *Teodramática 3. Las personas del drama: el hombre en Cristo*, Madrid 1993, 187. KARL RAHNER's affirmation that Christology is the beginning and the end of anthropology is well known. Cfr. among other places, «Para la teología de la encarnación» in *Escritos de Teología* IV, Madrid 1964, 133.

36 Cfr. IRENAEUS OF LYONS, *Adv. Haer.* V 6,2: «In past times it was said about man that he had been made in the image of God, but this was not so clear, as the Word, in whose image man had been created, was still invisible. So similarity was easily lost. But when the Word of God became flesh, he authenticated both things: He demonstrated the truth of the image, made in a person that was in his image, and he firmly established the similarity, jointly creating similar man to the invisible Father through the visible Word». Cfr. ORBE A., *Teología de san Ireneo* II, Madrid-Toledo 1987, 91-101.

b) Not only has God's design been revealed in the fullness of time, but humanity has opposed the divine design from the beginning. The step from the first Adam to the second and last Adam has not been a peaceful one. From the beginning, humanity has sinned and lost God's friendship. The coming of Christ as the new man brings newness to the old one (cfr. Rom 6:6; 2 Cor 5:17; Eph 4:22), a new and radical beginning made possible only by the obedience of Christ, which liberates us from the slavery of sin, a state that humanity, through its own power, would have never been able to overcome. In Christ we are a new creation because God has reconciled the world with himself (cfr. 2 Cor 5:17-18). Jesus is the one who takes away the sin of the world (cfr. John 1:29). A new beginning is necessary because humanity has not been faithful to the divine vocation which from the beginning guided him to Christ, although he would not have been able to know it. Christ, as he leads humanity to our vocation, liberates us from the slavery in which humanity has placed himself.

c) The effective newness of the coming of Christ, who brings salvation, is that he personifies wisdom, justice, righteousness, and redemption (1 Cor 1:30). Saint Irenaeus has magisterially formulated the meaning of newness in Christ, in spite of it being announced by prophets since ancient times:

> Read with earnest care that Gospel which has been conveyed to us by the apostles, and read with earnest care the prophets, and you will find that the whole conduct, and all the doctrine, and all the sufferings of our Lord, were predicted through them. But if a thought of this kind should then suggest itself to you, to say, What, then, did the Lord bring to us by his advent? Know ye that he brought all [possible] newness, by bringing himself who had been announced. For this very thing was proclaimed beforehand, that a newness should come to renew and quicken mankind … But when the King has actually come, and those who are his subjects have been filled with that joy which was proclaimed beforehand, and have attained to that liberty which he bestows, and share in the sight of him, and have listened to his words, and have enjoyed the gifts which he confers, the question will not then be asked by any that are possessed of sense what new thing the King has brought beyond [that proclaimed by] those who announced his coming. For he has brought himself, and has bestowed on men those good things which were announced beforehand, «into which angels long to look» (1 Pet 1:12)[37].

---

[37] IRENAEUS OF LYONS, *Adv. Haer.* IV 34,1.

It is Christ personally who brings salvation. Through his life, death, and resurrection, the announced salvation is realized. This is the core message of the New Testament. Furthermore, the reality of salvation is much greater than the announcement. In Christ there is the fullness of divinity, and we have all received of this fullness in order to be saved (cfr. Col 1:9-10; John 1:16). Only if Christ really becomes as we are may we become what he is, according to the old patristic *doctrine of exchange*[38]. Except for the freedom of God, who certainly could save us through other means, we have to insist that there path of salvation and human fullness is revealed through the incarnation of the Son, in whom the saving designs of God are fulfilled. It is his presence in the world —his life, death, and resurrection— that brings salvation, and therefore, the newness and perfection of humankind. Nothing other than this was intended by the early Church when it spoke of salvation being linked to this truth about humanity, and specifically regarding the incarnation of the Lord[39]. And to this same incarnation is linked the presence and the gift of the Spirit to humanity, once he had «become accustomed» to dwelling among humanity in the flesh of Christ[40]. Previously, in the time of the prophets, God had accustomed humanity simply to follow his Spirit and be in communion with him[41]. That was why the Spirit was communicated to us as the spirit of Jesus. Only the Spirit is capable of bringing humanity to divine sonship in and with Christ, which constitutes his destiny (cfr. Gal 4:6; Rom 8:14-16). This pouring out of the Spirit is also a dimension of the newness of Christ on which it depends[42].

---

[38] Cfr. IRENAEUS OF LYONS, *Adv. Haer.* III 19,1 (SCh 211, 374): «He who was the Son of God became the Son of man, that man, having been taken into the Word, and receiving adoption, might become the son of God … But how could we be joined to incorruptibility and immortality, unless, first, incorruptibility and immortality had become that which we also are…?». Cfr. also *Adv. Haer.* III 18,7 (366); IV 20,3; 33,4 (SCh 100, 634; 810); V *praef.* (SCh 153, 34). For other patristic references cfr. LADARIA L.F., *Teología del pecado original y de la gracia*, Madrid 2001, 151.

[39] IRENAEUS OF LYONS, *Adv. Haer.* III 10,3 (SCh 211,124): «Salutare autem quoniam Spiritus… Salus autem quoniam caro»; TERTULLIAN, *De res. mort.* VIII 2 (CCL 2,931): «Caro cardo salutis»; HILARY OF POITIERS, *In Mat.* 4,4 (SCh 254,132): «Ita corporalitas eius et passio voluntas Dei est et salus saeculi est».

[40] Cfr. IRENAEUS OF LYONS, *Adv. Haer.* III 17,1 (SCh 211,330): «Becoming accustomed in fellowship with Him to dwell in the human race, to rest with human beings, and to dwell in the workmanship of God, working the will of the Father in them, and renewing them from their old habits into the newness of Christ».

[41] Cfr. *Adv. Haer.* IV 14,2 (SCh 100, 542-544).

[42] The Fathers have bonded the newness of the risen Christ with the newness of the grace of the Spirit. Cfr. among others, IRENAEUS OF LYONS, *Adv. Haer.* III 17,1; ORIGEN, *De Princ.* I 3,7 (SCh 252,158); II 7,2 (SCh 328).

Evidently, the insistence on this newness of Christ and the fact that through Jesus comes salvation does not mean that salvation in the days before Christ did not depend on this event. The Son of God, anticipating his incarnation, had always been present among the human race[43]. In a mysterious way, the effects of the coming of Christ into the world were anticipated even before it happened. The only economy of salvation has as its unique center the incarnation of the Son, and its saving action is always realized through the Holy Spirit. The Spirit does not have a wider realm of action than that of Jesus. «Hence, the connection is clear between the saving mystery of the incarnate Word and that of the Spirit, who actualizes the saving efficacy of the Son made man in the lives of all people, called by God to a single goal, both those who historically preceded the Word made flesh, and those who live after his coming in history: the Spirit of the Father, bestowed abundantly by the Son, is the animator of all (cfr. John 3:34)»[44]. So the newness of Christ does not oppose the universality of his saving action. Only his unique newness can liberate the transitory quality that affects the whole of humanity.

3) The relationship between Christ and humanity presupposes that the latter has a true consistency as creature as well as true freedom, not in spite of, but by virtue of its bond to Christ[45]. The rediscovery in recent Catholic theology of the intimate relationship between the central function of Christ in salvation and in creation, has taken place, in some measure, due to the dialogue with the Christocentrism of Karl Barth, who in his time was considered by H. U. von Balthasar as a proponent of Christological reductionism (*christologische Engführung*)[46]. He himself showed how, even by the middle of the last century and much before Vatican II, the Christological view of the world and history was something already acquired in some milieus of Catholic theology[47]. Around that time and precisely in relation to the Council of Chalcedon, Karl Rahner proposed his well-known thesis to which we have referred[48]. The human nature of the Logos at-

---

43 Cfr. IRENAEUS OF LYONS, *Adv. Haer.* III 16,6; 18,1 (SCh 211,332;342): IV 6,7; 20,4; 28,2 (SCh 100,454; 634-636;758), V 16,1 (SCh 153,214); *Demons.* 12 (FP 2,81-82).

44 CONGREGATION FOR THE DOCTRINE OF THE FAITH, declaration *Dominus Iesus*, 12 (On the unicity and saving universality of Jesus Christ and the Church, Vatican, Rome 2000).

45 VON BALTHASAR H.U., *Teodramática 4. La acción*, Madrid 1995, 110. «God imagined and created the first Adam clearly in reference to the second one, but did not, even secretly, force the shape of the second on him».

46 Cfr. VON BALTHASAR H.U., *Karl Barth. Darstellung und Deutung seiner Theologie*, Cologne 1962, 371.

47 Cfr. VON BALTHASAR H.U., *Karl Barth. Darstellung und Deutung seiner Theologie*, 335-370.

48 Cfr. RAHNER K., «Problemas actuales de Cristología» in *Escritos de Teología* I, Madrid 1963.

tains its supreme degree of autonomy to the extent that it achieves radical proximity to God. On this basis we can follow our own reasoning: the destiny of humanity in Christ does not detract from his freedom or his human consistency. Rather, it grants it. The free response of humanity to God is justified in the face of reason: a Christian must always be ready to give reason for his hope (cfr. 1 Pet 3:15), and this response is even freer simply because it is founded in the obedience of Christ to the Father, in the response of the human volition of Jesus, which is the most free, as it is not at all polluted by sin and the slavery coming from sin. Thus, vocation in Christ and creaturely autonomy grow in the same proportion and cannot ever oppose each other. To establish the foundation of humanity's freedom in the acceptance of our vocation and destiny means that, effectively, our only vocation is the divine one, that our freedom is solely realized in the acceptance of what constitutes our fullness, and that, quite the reverse, its rejection, which is always possible, represents our dehumanization.

4) This rejection has been produced by human sin. Humanity has wished to be god based on its own strengths, to set our destiny outside of what the one God has designed for us. Thus, the coming of Jesus, in his newness, signifies the judgment of humanity and the world[49]. John's Gospel notably insists on this aspect (cfr. John 3:17-19; 5:22-27; 8:15-16; 12:31). All points made before are somehow summarized and focused here. On the one hand, Jesus can be judge and criterion for the judgment of humanity only because humanity has been called to fullness in him. Otherwise, it would make no sense for humanity to be judged by this principle. On the other hand, the newness of Christ appears to be highlighted here; only with the coming of Christ to earth may this judgment take place. This, at the same time, refers us to the judgment linked to the appearance of Christ in glory at his second coming (cfr. Matt 25:31-46)[50]. It is clear that it would not make sense to speak of judgment if the ability to respond in freedom did not exist in humanity, as well as the ability to close ourselves off from the divine calling. Under the merciful gaze of Jesus, humanity is able to discover the truth about itself.

Humanity is not the measure of Christ; rather, Christ is the measure of humanity and humanization. From Christology and nowhere else should anthropology extract its definitive criteria. Conformity with Christ is the ultimate

---

49 Cfr. KASPER W., «Christologie und Anthropologie» in *Theologische Quartalschrift* 162 (1982) 202-221.213. Article published in *Theologie und Kirche*, Maguncia 1987, 205-229.

50 For obvious reasons, we are not going into the relationship between the judgment involved in the first coming of the Lord and the one linked to his glorious manifestation at the end of times.

and definitive vocation of all humanity. But, at the same time, Christology presupposes an anthropology, even though it surpasses and is critical of it. In the encounter with Christ, humanity already knows something about itself, and if Christ may enlighten our condition, it is because he shares it with us. If at first humanity's movement is toward Christ, in the second stage it is Christ who reveals to humanity the ultimate reality about ourselves. He says it in part from without, because humanity can never on his own reach the meaning of the newness of Jesus. But this revelation cannot fail to find a profound meaning within the heart of humanity and in the depths of our intimate being, especially if we have been created in Christ and the fullness to which Christ invites us cannot be something solely extrinsic, without any relation to the depths of what he truly is. The creation of humankind in Christ and the unity of God's design, and the newness brought about by Christ are two equal aspects of the Christian message that must always be united in a fruitful tension.

Christian Anthropology as a Proposal for a New Humanism

The goal of this chapter is to assume a more or less precise idea of humanism[1], before which Christianity would offer something new that would be worthy of mentioning. Indeed, generally speaking, we would deem such a proposal as acceptable. First and foremost, Christianity believes in the transcendent destiny of humanity; thus, it will be close to, and will more easily dialogue with, those ways of thinking that sustain the dignity of the human being and its unique character among those who oppose reductive views of man[2], placing him, to the contrary, at the center of this concern, which does not renounce the issue regarding the meaning of his existence[3]. The Christian view of humanity will be in accordance with these criteria, although it will continue to offer specific elements that have faith in Jesus as their origin. This leads us to an initial welcome —not a rejection— of the values shared by people in our time. At first glance, Vatican II seems to point in this direction when it said at the beginning of the pastoral constitution *Gaudium et Spes:* «For faith throws a new light on everything, manifests God's design over man's total vocation, and thus directs the mind to solutions which are fully human. This council, first of all, wishes to assess in this light those values which are most highly prized today and to relate them to their divine source»[4]. It begins with the basis of shared values, which must be illuminated by a new light.

We speak about the dignity of the human being, of human rights, of humanism as a whole, without giving this word too precise a meaning, which clearly does not coincide with the meaning it had in the Renaissance and other historical periods. What *new* meaning does Christian anthropology bring *vis-à-vis* an ocean of approximations about humanity that makes the word «anthropology» one of the most ambiguous in our language today? What is the scope of this innovation? It is precisely this issue on which I wish to focus this presentation. For without disregarding all of the great and noble things humanity has been able

---

1 Cfr. LADARIA L.F., «La antropología cristiana como propuesta de un nuevo humanismo» in *Antropología y fe cristiana. IV Jornada de Teología,* Santiago de Compostela 2003, 193-221.

2 Toward the middle of the last century, humanism was vindicated by existentialist perspectives, such as: SARTRE J.P., *L'existentialisme est un humanisme,* Paris 1946; HEIDEGGER M., *Brief über den Humanismus,* Berna 1954. «Marxist Humanism» was also mentioned (cfr. RUIZ DE LA PEÑA J.L., *Muerte y marxismo humanista,* Salamanca 1976).

3 Cfr. ALFARO J., *De la cuestión del hombre a la cuestión de Dios,* Salamanca 1988; RUIZ DE LA PEÑA J.L., *Crisis y apología de la fe. Evangelio y nuevo milenio,* Santander 1995, 286-291.

4 *Gaudium et Spes* 11. The Council still affirmed, ibid., 12: «Believers and non-believers generally agree with this point: all of the earth's bounties ought to be ordained for the good of man, core and peak of them all». Perhaps the accord would not today be as broad in considering humanity as the core and peak of this world.

to conceive about itself, I think that the Christian view of the human being offers very definite and specific characteristics that represent a more radical uniqueness than there would initially appear to be.

1

Data from Biblical Anthropology

Let us begin with some brief references to the anthropology of the Old Testament. Already on its opening page, the Bible tells us that the human being, male and female, has been created by God in his image and likeness (cfr. Gen 1:26-27; 5:1; 9:6-7)[5]. In light of the fact of this unique dignity, the psalmist, probably aware of this priestly tradition, admiringly asks about this unheard-of privilege: «What are human beings that you are mindful of them, mortals that you care for them? Yet you have made them little lower than God, and crowned them with glory and honor… put all things under their feet» (Ps 8:4-6; cfr. Ps 144:3). The admiration is even greater, if one takes into account that humanity is a passing, ephemeral being, like a puff of smoke or a shadow passing by (cfr. Ps 144:4; 39:5-7; 62:10), which flowers one day and withers the next (cfr. Isa 40:6-7; Ps 40:5-6), and at the least expected moment will disappear from the earth, any trace of it forever lost in the relentless flow of history. Sirach also echoes this paradox: «The Lord created human beings out of the earth and makes them to return to it again. He gave them a fixed number of days, but granted them authority over everything on the earth. He endowed them with a strength like his own, and he made them in his own image» (Sir 17:1-3); and a bit later: «What are human beings, of what use are they?… Like a drop of water from the sea and a grain of sand, so are a few years among the days of eternity» (Sir 18: 8-10). Humanity, therefore, is a weak and fragile being, whom God has nevertheless made in the «image of his nature» (cfr. Wis 2:23).

The Old Testament does not hesitate to consider humanity to be the center of creation, and in whom is discovered the ultimate sense of what God has created. Everything God creates day by day, according to the first chapter in Genesis,

---

[5] At this time, we will not address the diverse interpretations of these texts, but I want to underscore how Vatican Council II, in *Gaudium et Spes* 12, has begun its anthropological argument while precisely making reference to that biblical teaching. It is the first time that this happens in an ecumenical council. This is, undoubtedly, very significant.

is «good». It becomes «very good» when on the sixth day the work of creation is completed with the appearance of humanity (cfr. Gen 1:4,10,18,21,25,31). According to the Yahwist's narrative of creation, humans are charged with the task of mastering all that God has made (cfr. Gen 2:15, 19-20). The paradox of greatness and misery, of the dignity and temporality of humanity, is not unraveled in the Old Testament. This paradox becomes even more evident if we take into account that the human being, besides being weak and ephemeral from the start, also appears as a sinner, disobedient to God, who has created and heaped honors on him (cfr. Gen 3:6; 4:8; 6:5-12) and who, in any case, does not abandon him (Gen 3:15; 8:21-22).

The statements in the Old Testament about humanity having been created in the image of God, crowned with glory and dignity, are applied in the New Testament to Jesus Christ. «He is image of the invisible God, firstborn of all of creation» (Col 1:15; cfr. 2 Cor 4:4; Phil 2:6; Heb 1:2-3). Ps 8:5-7 is cited in reference to Christ in Heb 2:6-8. What has been said in general about the dignity of humanity is now specifically said about a given man, Jesus. This elementary confirmation initially shows that Christian anthropology cannot be understood without an intrinsic reference to Christ. The uniqueness offered by Christian anthropology will therefore have to be linked essentially with the uniqueness of Christ.

And indeed, regarding Christ and his endeavor, the New Testament frequently uses the word «new»: a new covenant (cfr. Luke 22:20), a new wine (cfr. Mark 2:18), a new teaching (cfr. Mark 2:27), and the newness of the life of the spirit (cfr. Rom 6:4). The Christian person is a new creation (cfr. 2 Cor 5:17; Gal 6:15), and in Christ humanity is made new: «abolishing the law with its commandments and legal claims, that he might create in himself one new person in place of the two, thus establishing peace, and might reconcile both with God, in one body, through the cross» (Eph 2:15-16)[6]. Jesus himself taught his disciples to «put on the new self, created in God's way in righteousness and holiness of truth» (Eph 4:24). The «new man» —par excellence— does not exist except in Christ. Only in him can human beings become a new creation: «everything old has passed away; see, everything has become new» (2 Cor 5:17). These and other parallel

6 GNILKA J., *Der Epheserbrief*, Friburgo-Basilea-Viena 1971, 142: «Here Christ creates in himself. He is the universal man, who assumes in himself, unites and pacifies both, and humanity with them. With that there is no restitution of anything which existed before, but rather something new is realized, a new man». Ibid., 239, regarding the following text: «Human beings are not identical with Christ, but without a doubt, do have Christ as measure».

texts insist on transformation, the move from the old to the new, from the old man to the newness of Christ (cfr. Rom 6:6; Eph 4:22). Christ, because of his obedience unto death, has changed humanity as a whole, which he brings with him and in him from death to new life. Paul said in the letter to the Romans and in the first letter to the Corinthians with the parallel between Adam and Christ: «as one man's trespass led to condemnation for all, so one man's act of righteousness leads to justification and life for all» (Rom 5:18). «For since death came through a human being, the resurrection of the dead has also come through a human being; for as all die in Adam, so all will be made alive in Christ» (1 Cor 15:21-22). Therefore, the newness of Christ is, essentially, an overcoming of a situation of sin and death, of human slavery under the powers of evil. It is a liberation that the New Testament attributes to the Son and to truth (cfr. John 8:32-36), to Christ and his Spirit (cfr. 2 Cor 3:27; Gal 5:1).

Christian anthropology knows that humanity is not only fragile —the New Testament is as clear on this point as is the Old— but also a sinner who does not on his own have the possibility of overcoming this situation. The new man whom Christ creates in himself —and in his body, the Church— is the man whom Christ has saved from the slavery of sin while he has restored freedom to the children of God. Only insofar as man is the object of Christ's salvation and the recipient of the message of salvation does the New Testament deal with him. Anthropology is not the primary concern of Christian revelation. The first concern of Christian revelation is to show God to us, whom Christ reveals by saving us and at the same time giving us new life. But humanity is the recipient of this salvation and the message that God loves us and saves us in Christ. In this sense, and in this way, humanity becomes the second focus of an ellipse; he is the object of divine revelation as its recipient and above all as an object of the love of God. The admiration of the psalmist gives way to a greater admiration for the fact that God has so loved the world and humanity that he has sent the Son for our salvation. He has loved us first (cfr. John 3:16-17; 1 John 4:9-11, 19). The proof that God loves us is that, while we were still sinners, he sent his Son so that we would be reconciled with him (cfr. Rom 5:8, 10:2; Cor 5:19).

But the love of God for us does not depend on our sin. Sin, although it has undoubtedly determined the concrete form of its manifestation, is in no way a determinant of love itself. On the contrary, it is the love of God that determines humanity's being from the beginning, before there was sin. And the image and likeness in the Bible are before human sin. Did humanity only begin to relate to God once sin entered the picture? Wide schools of theological thought have held this view through centuries in the West. It is worthwhile to cite texts from Saint Augustine: «Si homo non perisset, Filius hominis non venisset»[7]. «Quare venit in mundum? Peccatores saluos facere. Aliam causa non fuit, quare veniret in mundum»[8]. It is not a matter of going back to disputes on the motive of the incarnation, even though they have some importance. This question has to do, very directly, with Christian anthropology. To what extent is Christ part of the definition of humanity? Does he come on stage only after humanity has fallen and is in need of a redeemer?

The New Testament does not directly respond to this query. But there are elements allowing us to formulate an answer. In the first place, it is about the parallel between Adam and Christ that has been previously mentioned. If, in some aspect, this important Pauline motive centers in the paradigm of sin-redemption or death-resurrection, it is not the only dimension that is underscored. In 1 Cor 15:45-49, the final destiny of humanity in the reproduction of the image of Christ links the first creation with the resurrection, without mentioning sin directly. If the first Adam is made a living soul, the second, Christ, is made spirit that gives life, so that, as we have borne the earthly image, so we would also bear the heavenly one. The first creation and the ultimate vocation of humanity are placed in intimate relationship. The latter is the completion of the former. The traits of the new man and the last Adam appear somehow designed at the moment when God forms the first Adam from the dust of the earth and breathes life

---

7   AUGUSTINE, *Sermo* 174, 2 (*Opere di Sant'Agostino* 31/2, 842).

8   AUGUSTINE, *Sermo* 174, 8 (*Opere*, 31/2, 850); *De pec. meritis et remissione* I 26,39 (*Opere*, 17/1,68): «…non aliam ob causam in carne venisse… nisi ut hac dispensatione misericordiosissimae gratiae omnes… vivificaret, salvos faceret, liberaret, redimeret, illuminaret, qui prius fuissent in peccatorum morte». Also *Sermo* 27,2 (*Opere*, 29,516); «Si enim sub captivitate non teneremur, redemptore non indigeremur».

into him, a foreshadowing of the gift of the Holy Spirit (cfr. Gen 2:7; John 20:22). Those he predestined he has called to conform to the image of his Son, so that he may be firstborn among many (cfr. Rom 8:29). We are guided to a similar conclusion by the hymn in the letter to the Ephesians: «even as he chose us in him before the foundation of the world, that we should be holy and blameless before him in love: he predestined us for adoption as sons through Jesus Christ, according to the purpose of his will, to the praise of his glorious grace, with which he has blessed us in the Beloved» (Eph 1:4-6). It is not a complete development of the idea; only traces of it are to be found[9]. But we cannot push it aside, especially if we keep in mind the developments that took place later on.

Indeed, what in Paul is only an intimation becomes explicit assertions at the end of the second century. In contrast with Gnostic views and Marcion's theology, which proposed creation as a fall and separated it from God's salvation in Christ, the Church had to defend the radical unity of the economy whose center is Christ. The New Testament had spoken of the creation of everything through Christ (cfr. 1 Cor 8:6; Col 1:15-16; Heb 1:2-3; John 1:3,10). The tragedy of sin cannot be forgotten, but this deed of such bitter consequences has not been able to destroy the radical goodness of everything created by God. Divine fidelity is always stronger than human sin. Humanity especially has continued to be the privileged object of the love of God. God, particularly through the constant proximity of his Son, has never abandoned us[10]. This closeness of the Son to humanity culminates in the incarnation, and from it we come to understand our ultimate purpose. We anticipated the coming of Christ before the Incarnation, as well as its immediate outcome after the ascension of the Lord into heaven, even knowing that the glorified Jesus continues to be present among us. In the creation of Adam, at the beginning of time, the Incarnation of the Word was already foreshadowed. Saint Irenaeus said:

> From this, then, whilst it was still virgin, God took dust of the earth and formed the man, the beginning of mankind. So then the Lord, summing up afresh this man, took the same dispensation of entry into flesh, being born from the Virgin by the will and

9   Joachim Gnilka in his comments on the Ephesians text, pinpoints that in references to the new man, one may find hints on the definitive realization in Gen 1:26. Cfr. GNILKA J., *Der Epheserbrief,* Friburgo-Basilea-Viena 1971, 239.

10 Above all, IRENAEUS OF LYONS has repeatedly insisted on the constant nearness of the Logos to mankind; cfr. *Adversus Haereses* III 16,6 (SCh 211,312): «semper aderat generi humano»; III 18,1 (SCh 342); IV 6,7 (SCh 100,454); 20,4 (634-636); 28,2 (758); V 16,1 (SCh 153,214); *Demonst.* 12 (FP 2,81-82).

the wisdom of God; that he also should show forth the likeness of Adam's entry into flesh and there should be that which was written in the beginning, man after the image and likeness of God. Thus, of this earth yet virgin, God took dust and shaped man, the start of the human race. To fulfill this man, the Lord took over its same bodily disposition, born of a Virgin by the will and wisdom of God, for him also to manifest his bodily identity with Adam's and in fulfillment of what had been written: man in image and likeness of God (cfr. Gen 1:26)[11].

Some of Tertullian's passages are even more impacting:

He [God] purposely adopted the plural phrase, «Let *us* make» and «in *our* image» (cfr. Gen 1:16); and «become as one *of us*» (cfr. Gen 3:22). For with whom did he make man? And to whom did he make him like? [The answer must be that] the Son on the one hand, who was one day to put on human nature; and the Spirit on the other, who was to sanctify man. With these he did then speak, in the unity of the Trinity, as with his ministers and witnesses. In the following text also, he distinguishes among the persons: «So God created humankind in his image; in the image of God he created them» (Gen 1:27). Why say «image of God?» Why not «his own image» merely, if he was only one who was the maker, and if there was not also One in whose image he made man? But there was One in whose image God was making man, that is to say, Christ's image, who, being one day about to become Man more surely and more truly so [*homo futurus certior et verior*], had already caused the man to be called His image, who was then going to be formed of clay— the image and similitude of the true and perfect Man[12].

And even in the fourth century Hilary of Poitiers said:

---

11 IRENAEUS OF LYONS, *Demonst.* 32 (FP 2,123); 22 (FP 106); *Adv. Haer.* III 22,3 (SCh 211,438): «Because of it Adam himself was called by Paul "the figure of him to come" (Rom 5:14). Indeed, the Word, artisan of all things, had sketched in him the future economy which would redress the Son of God». Cfr. also ibid., III 22,1 (SCh 211,432); v 16,2 (SCh 153,216).

12 *Adv. Praxean* XII 3-4 (Scarpat, 170-172). Also *De res. mort.* VI 3-5 (CCL 2,928): «In any shape given to dust, there was the thought of Christ who had to be man … What God sketched, he did in the image of God, that is, of Christ … Hence, that dust which already had the image of Christ to be incarnated, was not solely a work of God, but also a guarantee (of the incarnation to come)». *Adv. Marc.* v 8,1 (CCL 1,685): «Therefore, if it is the image of the Creator, he, looking at Christ his Word, who had to be man, said: "Let us make humankind in our image and likeness (Gen 1:26)"».

Adam, by his very name, foreshadows the birth of the Lord, as the Hebrew name of Adam, translated into Greek as «*ge pyrra*», in Latin means «earth of the color of fire» and the Scriptures tend to use the term «earth» for human body flesh. This [flesh] which in the Lord was born of the Virgin by the Spirit, transformed in a new shape foreign to itself, has been made in keeping with the spiritual glory, according to the Apostle: «The second man is from heaven» (1Cor 15:47), and is the heavenly Adam because the earthly Adam «is a type of the one who was to come» (Rom 5:14)[13].

The link established between the first and second Adam is the creation of the universe and humanity in particular through the Word. Still more decisive is the fact that in the first Adam, God has sketched the profile of the humanity of his Son, foreshadowing the incarnation. From this same viewpoint, the idea that the Son is the one to come in search of humanity, created in keeping with him, when he had gone astray and away from God by his sin, is coherent. So says Saint Athanasius: «Even so was it with the all-holy Son of God. He, the image of the Father, came and dwelt in our midst, in order that he might renew mankind made after himself, and seek out his lost sheep, even as he says in the Gospel: "I came to seek and to save that which was lost (Luke 19:10)"»[14]. Although the motive of the redemption and the liberation from sin is underscored here, it is clear that it is not at this point that humanity's relationship with God begins. Precisely the fact that Christ is the one who comes to redeem humanity is presented as a sign that the renewal brought by Christ is not limited to sin, but indeed means the realization of God's design from the beginning. Humanity is liberated by the one who is present in his creation, not only as a mediator, but also as a model. For reasons too long to be explained here, this doctrinal viewpoint was almost completely lost, at least in Western theology[15]. The connection with other doc-

13 *Trac. Myst.* 1, 2 (SCh 19 bis 76); translation into Spanish by AYÁN CALVO J.J., in HILARIO DE POITIERS, *Tratado de los misterios,* Madrid 1993, 38-40. For an analysis of the text: LADARIA L.F., *La cristología de Hilario de Poitiers,* Roma 1989, 28-30. It is to be particularly noted that Rom 5:14 quotes the Greek *typos* as *image,* instead of *form.* The relationship between the first and the second Adam thus appears much more precise, even while coexisting with other ideas. This Christological view of the image of God remained in the West during the fourth and fifth centuries. Cfr. PETER CHRYSOLOGUS, *Ser.* 117,1-2 (CCL 24A,709); GREGORY OF ELVIRA, *Trac. Orig.* XIV 25; XVI 22 (FP 9,344-372); AURELIUS PRUDENTIUS *Apoteosis,* v 309; 1040 (*Obras completas,* BAC, Madrid 1981, 200; 240). Some references on Eastern Theology in GROSSI V., *Lineamenta di antropologia patristica,* Roma 1983, 81-82.

14 ATHANASIUS OF ALEXANDRIA, *De incarnatione Verbi,* 14, 2 (SCh 199,315).

15 Cfr. LADARIA L.F., «El hombre creado a imagen de Dios» in SESBOÜÉ B. (ed.), *Historia de los dogmas 2. El hombre y su salvación,* Salamanca 1996, 75-115, esp. 75-93.

trinal elements of primary importance has helped to make these ideas remain implicitly present in many settings of Christian life.

The invitation of Christ to follow him, so visible in the Gospels (cfr. Mark 1:17; 2:14; 8:34-38; 17:21; John 8:12), leads us in the same direction and receives in the light of these considerations a fuller meaning. The salvation united to this following is the full realization of humanity, not something extrinsic to what man is in his deepest being. We can say the same of the different passages in which the configuration of the risen Christ, expressed with different formulas, is seen as the fullness to which we are called (cfr. Rom 8:29; 1 Cor 15:49; 2 Cor 3:18; Gal 4:19; Col 2:12; 3:4). Hans Urs von Balthasar has clearly said that «the mediating function emerges also in creation, not only of the Logos but of Christ. This means that all things could only have been made in reference to their consummation in the second Adam, which is made perceptible solely in the being and consciousness of the Son who brings to completion his task. Once more, no other instance but the Creator could have placed him in this role of author of the consummation; if it were not so, he would not be able to do it *from within*, but would have to stamp his final mark *from without* on the things that had been created with a different origin»[16]. What is generically proposed here regarding creation has, in humanity's case, a specific application, because it is not only a matter of God making perfect in Christ what he has always thought of him and for him, but that Jesus, becoming human like us, brings to perfection our human nature because he is man like us, as he assumes our condition. He can only perfect it «from within» if from the very beginning of creation God had created us bearing in mind the incarnation of his Son. Tertullian's text —cited above— is enlightening. He is the *homo certior et verior*. We are human beings in the fullest and truest sense of the word to the extent that we assimilate ourselves to him.

---

16 VON BALTHASAR H.U., *Teodramática 3. Las personas del drama: el hombre en Cristo*, Madrid 1993, 237-238. PANNENBERG W.B., *Teología Sistemática* II, Madrid 1996, 25, offers similar views: «The affirmation of the mediation of the Son in creation, must be understood here (Heb 1:2; Col 1:16-20; Eph 1:10), from the start, in a *final* sense. This means that only in Jesus Christ the creation of the world shall be consummated. But as correct as this idea may be… the creative mediation of the Son cannot be limited to this aspect. The final ordering of creatures to the manifestation of Jesus Christ rather supposes that creatures have in the Son the origin of their being and their existence. Otherwise, the final recapitulation of all things in the Son (Eph 1:10) would be other than things themselves, which would mean that it would be the definitive recapitulation of the authentic being of created realities». The principle specifically applies to humankind in ibid., 245-247: «The intention of the Creator cannot be placed so inefficiently and extrinsic regarding His creature».

Christ and Humankind in Vatican II and Contemporary Theological Reflection

3.1. CHRIST, PERFECT IN HUMANITY

The Second Vatican Council has been a great doctrinal advancement in the field of theological anthropology, not only for what it has explicitly said, but also for what it has hinted at. The dogmatic development during the first centuries of the Church insisted on the perfection of the divinity and the humanity of Christ. The soteriological motives that pushed the development of Christological dogma, in strong connection with the Trinitarian dogma, were caused by the assertion at the Council of Chalcedon of his consubstantiality with us in his humanity, which followed the assertion at the Nicea Council about the consubstantiality of the Son and the Father (cfr. DH 301; already in the «Symbol of the Union»: DH 271-273). Only if Jesus, the eternal Son of God, has assumed our human condition in its integrity, has our salvation been real and complete. But this «perfection» of humanity, in the primary sense of complete humanity, is already slowly hinting at something more: the significance of paradigmatic humanity. Chalcedon already begins to note that this humanity is without sin. Obviously, this does not mean that something is missing, but rather that there is in Christ a perfection not found in us: a perfection that, far from distancing him from our condition, allows him to unite more intimately with it, because, in obedience to the Father's will, it allows him to shoulder upon himself the sins of all, and thus redeem us from the slavery that they bring about. When the Third Council of Constantinople affirmed the human volition of Jesus, in everything subordinated to the divine will, which is one with the will of the Father, it insisted on this notion of the perfection of the humanity of Christ; precisely by virtue of his unique and unrepeatable communion with God in the hypostatic union, this humanity does not remain either absorbed or diminished, but rather elevated and empowered to the maximum in its creaturely autonomy. *Humana augens* (DH 293) is the beautiful formula by Saint Leo the Great on the eve of the dogmatic definition of Chalcedon, to which he greatly contributed. The greater proximity to God brings greater completeness to human beings, never the opposite[17]. And it

---

17 Cfr. RAHNER K., «Problemas actuales de cristología» in *Escritos de Teología* I, Madrid 1963 169-222. On page 183: «Radical dependence on God does not grow in inverse ratio but in a direct one, with true autonomy before him». COMISIÓN TEOLÓGICA INTERNACIONAL, *Documentos 1969-1996*,

is obvious, on the other hand, that this perfection does not mean an abstract measure to which Christ would conform in an eminent fashion. The perfect man is Christ, and in him —and only in him— is the meaning of the perfection of humanity discovered.

The Second Vatican Council's formulations, although they do represent a notable doctrinal development, are not a radical novelty, thus *Gaudium et Spes* 22, in particular:

> The truth is that only in the mystery of the incarnate Word does the mystery of man take on light. For Adam, the first man, was a figure of him who was to come, (cfr. Rom 5:14)[18], namely Christ the Lord. Christ, the final Adam, by the revelation of the mystery of the Father and his love, fully reveals man to man himself and makes his supreme calling clear… He who is *the image of the invisible God* (Col 1:15) is himself the perfect man. To the sons of Adam he restores the divine likeness which had been disfigured from the first sin onward. Since human nature as he assumed it was not annulled, by that very fact it has been raised up to a divine dignity in our respect too. For by his incarnation the Son of God has united himself in some way with every person[19].

It is not a matter of making a literal comment on this passage, but rather of underscoring some of the themes burgeoning within it. First, there is the fundamental meaning of Christ for Christian anthropology. Only the mystery of the incarnate Word sheds light on the mystery of humanity; Christ reveals humanity to itself. Many valid things have been said about humanity from various perspectives, and indeed, the Council does not propose to undo or ignore them. But the question derives, in all its radicalism, from the text: what does the fact of the incarnation of the Son mean for the definition of humanity? Does it simply

---

POZO C., S.J. (ed.) BAC, Madrid 1998, I E) 4, Madrid 1998, 254: «In the same manner as the incarnation of the Word does not move nor diminish divine nature, neither does the divinity of Jesus Christ move or dissolve human nature, rather it affirms it more and perfects it in its original creaturely condition… The more deeply Jesus Christ lowers himself into human misery, the higher can man participate in divine life».

18 Also cited TERTULLIAN, *De res. mort. (De carnis resurrectione)*, 6: «Quodcumque limus exprimebatur; Christus cogitabatur, homo futurus».

19 Cfr. meaningful quotes of this text in JOHN PAUL II, *Redemptor hominis* 8; *Fides et Ratio* 60, where the Pope himself says that this text is one of the constant references in his teachings. The same JOHN PAUL II, in *Fides et Ratio* 80, says: «Only here the meaning of existence reaches its peak. It becomes intelligible, in effect, the intimate essence of God and of man in the mystery of the incarnate Word, divine nature and human nature, with its respective autonomy are safeguarded while the unique liaison in this mutual relationship is shown without any confusion».

show us —which is already much more than we human beings on our own would have been able to think— the depth of God's love for humanity? Or does it also tell us what humanity really is at the deepest level?

In Catholic theology, Karl Barth's strong and somewhat radical ideas have been added to the debate with great vigor and in an expressive way: only beginning with Christ do we know who and what humanity is, while we know who and what God is beginning with humanity[20]. Catholic theology has equally clear viewpoints on a more positive evaluation of creation, precisely in the light of Christ. Karl Rahner developed his thesis on creation and in fact on human being's creation as the «grammar» of a possible divine self-communication. It is the language God creates to be able to freely express and communicate the salvific truths of which he himself is the content. In this sense, the possibility of creation as the beginning of God's manifestation —and as a measure also of his self-revelation— would rest on the possibility of the occurrence and radical «disrobing» of the incarnation. This does not mean that creation cannot be without incarnation, or that humanity could not exist without the incarnation of the Son. The only affirmation is that they could not be without the *possibility* of incarnation, which is something else entirely. The opposite would deny the freedom of the incarnation and nature, and the world would be confused with grace and the communication God offers of himself.

It is the possibility of the greater that gives foundation to the lesser, and not the other way around. It is God's ability to assume, to become what he is not, that establishes the capacity to create out of nothingness. The humanity of Jesus is created when the Son assumes it. It does not have a prior existence, neither chronologically nor logically. Because God is able to assume and create, he can create without assuming. Because he is able to express himself and utter his definite word of love in the incarnation of his Son, he can manifest himself in creation. The definition of human being itself is understood from this perspective: it is what emerges when God's self-expression, his Word, is uttered in love in the vacuum of the nothingness without God *(in das Leere des gott-losen Nichts)*. From the beginning there were human beings, because the Son of Man had to come.

---

20 BARTH K., *Kirchliche Dogmatik* 3/2, Munich, 13: «Wer und was der Mensch ist, dass wird uns im Worte Gottes nicht weniger bestimmt und dringlicher gesagt wie dieses, wer und was Gott ist»; «Eben Mensch ist ja Gott selber in der vollkommenen und entgültigen Offenbarung dieses Wortes geworden». VON BALTHASAR H.U., *Karl Barth. Darstellung und Deutung seiner Theologie*, Cologne 1951, 335-344, among other places.

Humanity is what emerged when God wanted to be no-God. Every human being is thus, in the deepest way possible, a potential brother or sister of Jesus[21]. Hans Urs von Balthasar has dealt with the question in a similar way: God says yes to creation, even when creation may respond negatively to the Creator. Also, the relationship between God and humanity is founded in divine life, in the infinite distance between the Father and the Son in the inseparable union of the Holy Spirit[22]. He has also used the terminology of *grammar* to express the relationship between creation and God's self-expression in the incarnation: «Natural man knows what is ethics and practical reason, and Old Testament man also knows what ought to be the just relationship with the living God. In this grammar, Jesus can record the word of God»[23]. And again, without using the term, he expresses the idea more clearly: «God has created the creature in his image and likeness so that said creature through grace may be able, from within, to serve as sounding board through which God may express himself and be understood»[24].

Beginning with these theological interpretations, these affirmations —necessarily more generic in *Gaudium et Spes*— may be further fleshed out. Christ unveils who the human is because the principle source of his creation clearly appears. There are human beings, within the concrete economy in which we move, because Christ had to exist. If the possibility of the creation of humanity is founded in the possibility of incarnation, it is obvious who the model is from which humanity has been sketched, and with it a new definition of the human being: that which God becomes when he does not become God. According to the cited theologians, the creation of man in the image and likeness of God is thus a type of grammar[25] that allows God's self-expression. Christ is not seen beginning with Adam, but rather Adam is seen from the beginning of Christ, in spite of the important role played by the sin of Adam, the «first man». Hans Urs von Balthasar says that one is a «person» —in a full theological sense— upon being

---

21 Cfr. RAHNER K., *Grundkurs de Glaubens. Einführung in den Begriff des Christentums,* Friburgo-Basilea-Viena 1976. Karl Rahner has offered these ideas in his article «Para la teología de la encarnación» in *Escritos de Teología* IV, Madrid, 1964, 139-157.

22 Cfr. CORDOVILLA A., *Gramática de la encarnación. La creación en Cristo en la teología de K. Rahner y Hans Urs von Balthasar,* Madrid 2004, 451-453.

23 VON BALTHASAR H.U., *Theologik II. Wahrheit Gottes,* Einsiedeln 1985, 73.

24 VON BALTHASAR H.U., *Theologik II. Wahrheit Gottes, bid.* 76.

25 KASPER W., *Jesús el Cristo,* Salamanca 1975, 6. Kasper used the concept of grammar, although with a different meaning. Creation and, specifically, humanity is a grammar subject with multiple nuances. Elsewhere in the same work his position becomes more blended and more in keeping with that of other cited theologians; cfr. ibid., 237-238; 263-265. Similarly, see his article «Christologie und Anthropologie» in *Theologische Quartalschrift* 162 (1982) 202-221.

part of the mission of Christ, in whom his person and his mission are identified because his being is pure reference to the Father (and the Holy Spirit), and his obedience to the mission given in the economy of salvation is the transposition within the economy of salvation and the meaning of his being in divine eternity[26]. It is clear that this conclusion can be reached only because the apostles have seen and heard and passed their testimony onto the Church, starting with the concrete figure of Jesus of Nazareth, Lord and Christ. Jesus is necessarily placed at the core of the Christian view of humanity. Indeed, through his life and revelation of the Father, he reveals humanity to itself. He is the perfect man and not only «perfectly man». Both in patristic theology and in contemporary developments, there are elements fulfilling the contents of this expression. «Whoever follows Christ, the perfect man, becomes more of a man»[27], even «more human». The perfection of the humanity of Christ certainly goes beyond the simple condition of complete humanity, and even beyond moral perfection. In Christ's human nature, because it is assumed by the divine person, a unique dignity is attained (let us recall Saint Leo's *humana augens*) «also in us»: it is another significant statement of the Council. The «perfection» of our humanity, therefore, consists of participation in the perfection that flows from Christ. Vatican II proposes that the reason for this communication resides in the fact that the Son of God has joined, through the incarnation, all human beings. The text pinpoints «in some way» *(quodammodo)* so as not to compromise the character, which is absolutely unique and unrepeatable, of the hypostatic union. We do not have a term or formula to express this truth. Hence, there is a vagueness, certainly not a casual one, in the formulation. But the Council reminds us of a very important truth, with clear roots in the New Testament (cfr. Matt 25:31). Patristic theology has developed these ideas with much diversity of nuances. I will gladly cite a passage from Cyril of Alexandria in his commentary on John's Gospel (John 1:14):

> He says … that while also revealing this sublime mystery, the Word also dwells in us. Because we are all in Christ, each common person of humanity enjoys in himself Christ's life … Thus the Word has dwelled in us so that after the only Son of God has been formed in power, his dignity shall be poured out, in keeping with the Holy Spirit

26 Cfr. VON BALTHASAR H.U., *Teodramática 3. Las personas del drama: el hombre en Cristo*, Madrid 1993, 190-195.
27 *Gaudium et Spes* 41.

(cfr. Rom 1:4), on the whole of humanity, and hence, through each of us, we would get to those words: «You are gods and all children of the Most High» (Ps 82:6; John 10:34) … Is it not clear to all that he lowered himself to the nature of servant, without getting any advantage from this condition, and that he delivered himself for us so that we would be enriched through his poverty (cfr. 2 Cor 8:9) and through his own inexpressible goodness … raising us through his likeness with him and making us, through faith, gods and children of God? He, whose nature is the Son of God, has dwelled in us. Thus, in his Spirit, we exclaim «Abba, Father» (Rom 8:15; Gal 4:6). The Word dwells in all as his temple, namely, in what the Word assumes in us and for us, so that everyone who takes refuge him, he would reconcile in one body, in the words of Paul[28].

There are two important points here that are intimately connected. On the one hand, the incarnate Son constitutes the beginning of humanity and its sole foundation. Jesus is man *par excellence*; in him God's design for humanity is perfectly realized, and starting with this realization the whole of humanity makes sense. All of humanity shares in this fullness and are human beings because they are part of it. This realization of humanity is based on following Jesus and sharing in his mission. «Humanity», in each one of us, grows to the extent to which union with Christ increases. Participation in this fullness of Christ is founded on the fact that the Son of God, upon assuming the concrete humanity of Jesus, has mysteriously bonded with each of us. The worthiness that the divine person of the Son grants the assumed humanity is also communicated to us, because he has joined with everyone upon becoming a human being and sharing our condition. Every human being, therefore, is in a mysterious relationship with Christ. Theology should still seek to unveil this mystery, to shed light on the meaning of this union of the Son with all of humanity and with each of one of us[29], which certainly does not mean that humanity in each of us would be personalized by the Word. As it clearly hints in the text of Cyril of Alexandria, the Holy Spirit has a function here. The Spirit of holiness coming from Christ flows to form one body. The Word is the light, who, upon coming

---

28 CYRIL OF ALEXANDRIA, *In Johannis evangelium* I 9 (PG 73, 161-164). Some biblical texts from HILARY OF POITIERS are especially clear on this: *Tr. Ps.* 51,16 (CCL 61-104): «naturam in se uniuersae carnis adsumpsit»; 54,9 (146): «uniuersitatis nostrae caro est factus».

29 This Vatican II Council formulation is more concrete than those of the early fathers. The union with each human being is underscored and not solely in the abstract with the whole of humanity. Also, the concrete conditions in which Christ lived in the likeness of other human beings are added: «He labored with male hands, he thought with human intelligence, he behaved with human volition, he loved with a human heart» (*Gaudium et Spes* 22).

to the world, sheds light on every human being, (cfr. John 1:9) and we have all received this fullness. Keeping in mind everything we have said, this expression may already be applied in some fashion to the human creaturely condition, although it is obvious that it attains a fuller meaning when one considers the abundance of the supernatural gifts that the Lord has bestowed on us by making us participants in his own divine life.

In Christ, God's incarnate Word, we have thus the fullest realization of the human being. If, as we have remarked, the incarnation does not mean the reduction or the disappearance of human nature, but rather its peak realization, then likewise, in each of us, the proximity of Christ entails the greatest possible growth of our creaturely being, inasmuch as it is different from God, although dependent on him. Christocentrism, as observed in the tradition of the early Church and in modern attempts at Catholic theology, does not erase the human being by underscoring its reference to Christ. The great merit of the theologians we have cited has been to maintain creation and incarnation together, while at the same time retaining their essential differentiation. The fact that the latter endows the former with meaning shows us the deep unity of God's design, which has its sole center in Christ and which goes from creation to the final consummation. But there is more than a unity of design. Already in creation and in the conservation of everything through his Word, according to the Second Vatican Council, God gives to humanity a perennial witness of himself (cfr. *Dei Verbum* 3). In the creation of the world, and particularly that of humanity, God begins to express himself, while he creates the conditions for the fullness of his manifestation. Therefore, this manifestation occurs in the nature God granted to humanity —and not in spite of it— in the potentialities of it being given by God at the moment of his creation, not in the wiping out of these potentialities. However, it is also obvious that only God can realize these possibilities. Hence, it would be a contradiction to consider God and humanity as rivals or adversaries.

To think of Christ as the perfect man or of creation as the grammar of divine revelation is the peak assessment of nature and not ever its elimination. In this sense, theology cannot bypass dialogue with philosophy or human sciences, and their findings may very well nurture it. Because everything has been created through Christ, in no way does it follow that, starting with Christ, we may be able to know the entirety of this reality which makes sense only in regard to him. Even more, the human effort to know and deepen this truth, within our natural means, cannot hinder the comprehension of the Christian message.

John Paul II says in his Encyclical *Fides et Ratio* 73, that if the word of God is truth (cfr. John 17:17), the human search for truth should assist in the understanding of the word of God. The encyclical concretely refers —in its context— to philosophy. It should be mentioned that the established principle may apply to other sciences or fields of study related to it. Likewise, a better knowledge of this «grammar» may help us to better grasp the message that is offered. What the wisdom of centuries tells us about human beings is not something to be discarded by Christian anthropology. Church Fathers, since early times, used Greek philosophy in diverse ways and with different emphases.

Human beings did not receive from Christ our first idea about God. God has always been known because of creation (Wis 13:1-9; Rom 1:19-20). The coming of Christ has been prepared by revelation in the Old Testament, and Christ himself expressly referred to it. Similarly, many truths about humanity, known long before Christianity, have been assumed by the latter. In any case, it is conclusive that the revelation of Christ and his very person give these truths their fullest meaning. They are lit up with a new light. They are purified from blends of error or perversion. It is not in vain that Vatican II, whose teachings are fundamental references in this writing, has spoken of Christ as the new man and as the perfect man[30]. Both aspects go together. It is a perennial memory of the fact that the «perfection» of Jesus came about through his suffering and obedience to the Father (cfr. Heb 2:10; 5:8-9), thus overcoming the effects of Adam's disobedience.

The perfection of Jesus in the New Testament must be given its due weight. The first Adam has meaning in light of the second one, but the path from one to the other has not been peaceful. Humanity's sin and rejection of the divine plan lies in between. Hence, the cross, freely accepted in obedience to the Father, is part of this path. The perfection of humanity, in following Christ, also entails the acceptance of suffering. «In Christ God reconciled us with himself (cfr. 2 Cor 5:18; Col 1:1, 20-22) and with ourselves and freed us from the slavery of the devil and of sin, for which anyone of us can say with the Apostle: "The Son of God who loved me and gave himself for me" (Gal 2:20). Suffering for us, he gave us the example for us to follow in his steps (cfr. 1 Pet 2:21; Matt 16:24; Luke 14:27),

---

30 *Christ, the New Man* is the title of no. 22, which we have been citing. Precisely to underscore the newness embodied by the appearance of Christ for all people, this title was given to replace the previous one, *Christ, the Perfect Man.* Cfr. GERTLER T., *Jesus Christus. Die Antwort der Kirche auf die Frage nach dem Menschsein. Eine Untersuchung zu Funktion und Inhalt der Christologie im ersten Teil der Pastoralkonstitution «Gaudium et Spes» des Zweitens Vatikanischen Konzils,* Leipzig 1986. We have already seen the expression in this text.

and he also opened the way, and in following him, life and death are sanctified and gain new meaning» (*Gaudium et Spes* 22). Therefore, it should not be strange to hear of two linked aspects, which, each in its own way, propose salvation and fulfillment for Christians: conforming to the image of the Son, firstborn among many, and conforming with his death in order to reach resurrection[31]. It is the concrete path of discipleship proposed by the Gospels.

Christian anthropology does not offer us merely the image of the Christian man or a mere humanism, but also the Christian perspective of *humanity and humankind itself.* Every human being has been created in the image and likeness of God, and the vocation to reproduce the image of the risen Christ is extended to every one of us. Humanity has only one origin, and there is only one goal and one possible salvation for humanity. This is a direct consequence of the universal mediation of Jesus, reiterated so many times in the New Testament

(cfr. 1 Tim 2:4, 6; Heb 4:12; John 14:6). *Gaudium et Spes* also echoes this fundamental truth[32]. Hence, because «Christ died for all (cfr. Rom 8:32) and the supreme vocation of man is indeed only one, that is, divine ... we ought to believe that the Holy Spirit offers everyone the possibility that, in the manifested form of God, they may be associated with this paschal mystery»[33]. This notion of universality cannot go unnoticed by Christian anthropology. It should be seen regarding one point, which we have yet to make explicit: the condition of man as son.

3.2. HUMANITY'S DIVINE SONSHIP AS GOD'S CHILDREN

At the beginning of our cited text we were told that Jesus manifests humanity «in the same revelation of the mystery of the Father and of His love». These words deserve further comment. In his revelation of God as his Father, Jesus reveals himself in a very unique fashion, as the Son. Within the multiplicity of Christological titles in the New Testament, that of «Son» or «Son of God» has been considered, from early times and in all of the Church's tradition, as the one best expressing the ultimate identity of Jesus. It is easy to understand this preference:

31 *Gaudium et Spes* 22, 4: «Christians, conformed to the image of the Son, who is firstborn among many brethren (cfr. Rom 8:29; Col 3:10-14), receives *the first fruits of the Spirit* (Rom 8:23), endowing him to fulfill the new law of love... The need and duty to struggle is urgent for Christians, through many tribulations, against the devil, even to the point of death. In association with the paschal mystery, shaped by the death of Christ, he will reach the resurrection reaffirmed by hope (cfr. Phil 3:10; Rom 8:17)».

32 Cfr. above all *Gaudium et Spes* 10; 45.

33 *Gaudium et Spes* 22, 5. Elsewhere in this document, with diverse expressions, divine vocation is proposed as the only one for all humanity (*Gaudium et Spes*, 24; 29; 92).

it is the label that most directly shows the unique and unrepeatable relationship of Jesus with God. Already in the Old Testament one could think that, indeed, it is this relationship that determines the depths of being in each person, created in the divine image and likeness. And already in speaking of the future Messiah, the descendant of David, the divine Sonship has been expressed (cfr. 2 Sam 7:14; 1 Chr 22:10; Ps 2:7; 89:27).

The same metaphor of fatherhood and sonship has been used to express God's predilection for the people of the covenant (cfr. Exod 4:22-23; Deut 14:1-2; 32:5-6; Isa 1:2-3; 30:1-9). In the life of Jesus, divine fatherhood, and therefore his own sonship, acquire new connotations, which already appear during his earthly existence (the invocation of God as «Abba») and which are revealed, above all, beginning with the resurrection. Thus, John's writings can speak of Jesus as the only and beloved Son (cfr. John 1:14, 18; 3:6, 18; 1 John 4:9). Nonetheless, this begotten Son has taught his disciples to call God «Father» and to consider themselves as his children (cfr. Matt 6:42; Luke 12:30; Matt 5:43-48; Luke 6:32; 12:32), although the relationship of Jesus as Son of God and our own sonship are never seen as being equal in the New Testament. The revelation that Jesus makes upon revealing God as Father is thus a revelation of the calling to divine sonship as participants in the original Sonship of Jesus. Here, we may make a parallel anthropological consideration with the Christological one: among the many expressions used in the New Testament to express the condition of the new man saved by Jesus —the new man *par excellence*— due prominence is given, precisely because of our link to Christ and ultimately to God the Father, to the title «son of God». The ultimate identity of Jesus is as the Son of God; this is also our ultimate identity, through our participation in the original and unrepeatable Sonship of Christ, which is pure divine grace and gift. While begotten, he is the firstborn among many (cfr. Rom 8:29). The power of divine love allows for these two apparent contradictions to be perfectly compatible. In his incarnation the Son becomes our brother. He who believes in him is born of God. He has been begotten to new life, and thus in a very real sense becomes a son of God (cfr. 1 John 2:29-31; 3:9-10; 4:7; 5:1; 4:18). Divine sonship is made possible by the Holy Spirit, the Spirit of God and of Christ, who lives in us and through whom we may call out, «Abba, Father» (cfr. Rom 8:15; Gal 4:6), just as Jesus did (cfr. Mark 14:36)[34].

---

34 For more on this question, cfr. LADARIA L.F., *Teología del pecado original y de la gracia*, BAC, Madrid 2004, 236-244.

Everyone is called, without exception, to the divine Sonship of Jesus. *Gaudium et Spes* 22, in an immediate connection regarding what has been signified as the possibility given by the Holy Spirit to incorporate everyone and everything into the paschal mystery, concludes the following: «This is the great mystery of man which Christian revelation makes clear to the faithful … Christ is risen, and with his death he destroyed death and gave us life so that, as children in the Son, we could claim in the Spirit: *Abba, Father* (Rom 8:15; Gal 4:6)»[35].

The divine fatherhood and the ensuing sonship and brotherhood among humanity will never be underscored sufficiently. God behaves as Father of all when he makes rain fall and the sun shine over the just and the unjust alike, that is, on everyone (cfr. Matt 5:45). Many reasons may be found to consider the unity of the great human family. We may share in the common heritage of «Adam» (without discussing how this origin should be interpreted), within our social nature, or in the multiple liaisons binding people together, for good or evil, even in countries that are geographically distant from each other. None of these motives, no matter how significant they may be, will ever establish true brotherhood among human beings. This brotherhood is to be found only in the divine fatherhood, and is ours solely through our union with Jesus, who by nature is the only Son. That we may all be one body in him constitutes the divine plan for the human race, «to do everything which may have Christ as head, what is in heaven and what is on earth» (Eph 1:10)[36]. This is the strongest bond of unity among rational people. In this common vocation in Christ as members of his body, there is the deepest liaison of solidarity between human beings. Our relationship of sonship with the Father, in union with Jesus, cannot be lived except in brotherhood among human beings.

---

35 COMISIÓN TEOLÓGICA INTERNACIONAL, *Documentos 1969-1996*, POZO C., S.J. (ed.) BAC, Madrid 1998, I E) 3, 253: «Humankind, which has been created in the image and likeness of God, is invited to the communion of life with God, who is the only one able to fulfill the deepest desires of humanity. The idea of deification reaches its peak in the incarnation of Jesus Christ: the incarnate Word assumes our mortal flesh so that we, liberated from sin and death, may participate in divine life. Through Jesus Christ in the Holy Spirit we are children and co-heirs (cfr. Rom 4:17), "sharing in divine nature" (2 Pet 1:4). Divinization consists of this grace, which liberates us from death and sin and communicates divine life itself: we are sons and daughters in the Son». According to the teaching of the church fathers, the Son of God became son of man so that human beings would become, through him, the children of God. Cfr. for example, IRENAEUS OF LYONS, *Adv. Haer.* III 10,2; 19,1 (SCh 211,116-118; 374).

36 *Ad gentes* 7: «Thus, finally, the design of the Creator is fulfilled, who created man in his image and likeness, when everyone who participated in human nature regenerated in Christ by the Holy Spirit, together in contemplation of God's glory may be able to say "our Father"».

Jesus calls his disciples brothers and sisters (cfr. Mark 3:34-35; Matt 25:40; 28:10; John 20:17; Rom 8:29; Heb 2:11,12,17). Therefore, in Jesus, a new relationship among us is founded —indeed, one of *brotherhood*. Humanity's divine vocation in Christ is unique, and all human beings are called to it. The ultimate destiny of humanity cannot stray from our condition of sonship in relation with God, the Father of Jesus, whose divine fatherhood embraces everything (cfr. Eph 3:14; 4:6). Thus, we cannot call God Father if we do not behave as *brothers and sisters toward all*[37]. Jesus himself hints at a similarity between the union of divine persons and the union of his disciples with the Trinity: «That they all may be one. As you, Father, are in me and I am in you, may they also be in us ... the glory that you have given to me I have given them, so that they be one as we are one» (John 17:21-22). Vatican Council II, by echoing this idea, indicates that, by virtue of this similarity, humanity cannot find perfection other than by giving ourselves to others through brotherhood[38].

3.3. CHRIST, THE MEASURE OF HUMANKIND

The divine *sonship* of humanity and its subsequent bond of *brotherhood* with others is the radical newness of Christian anthropology. Founded in the newness of Christ, the divine plan of saving all in him, is, therefore, not deducible from any imaginable human presupposition. But this does not mean that this ultimate destiny may come to us «from without». On the contrary, it responds to what —from eternity— was in God's design, which was set into motion from the first moment of creation. Hence, from the Christian viewpoint, any definition of humanity that does not directly entail the ultimate end to which we are destined is not fully satisfactory. «In the very concept of man there ought to be a place for God's designs on him»[39]. Otherwise, we cannot fathom the depths of the ultimate meaning of humanity, which God has created and loved. Precisely because creation was done in Christ, and because humanity has from the beginning borne the mark of Christ, we may discover —and, in fact, have discovered throughout history, even without knowing of the revelation of Christ— truths that shed light on the dignity of our being, our transcendent destiny, our supe-

---

37 *Nostra aetate* 5: «We cannot call God Father of all if we do not want to behave as brethren with some people, created in the image of God. The attitude of man towards God the Father and the relationship of man towards his human brethren are bonded in such manner that, as Scripture says, *whoever does not love does not know God* (1 John 4:8)».
38 Cfr. *Gaudium et Spes* 24.
39 ORBE A., *Antropología de San Ireneo,* Madrid 1969, 20.

riority regarding the world around us, and the moral law written in the depths of our heart[40].

The truest knowledge of ourselves comes to us from our faith in Jesus, which on our own we would never be able to attain. On the other hand, we cannot but find a deep echo of this reality in our heart, which not even sin and the power of evil have been able to silence completely. In Christ's love of God and his fellow human beings, which was so deep that he gave his life for them, the message of the Beatitudes—Christ's self-portrait—[41] as well as the love he had for his enemies, and in the sincerity and wholesome fortitude of his life, humanity discovers the model to follow for our own realization, while at the same time becoming aware of the distance between the ideal and the reality.

The vision of humanity that the Christian message offers us, precisely because it finds its center in Jesus, who has come into the world to save us, gives us cause to work toward greater solidarity with every human being and the whole of humanity. These are the concerns that emerge from the initial chapters in *Gaudium et Spes*[42], today one of the necessary points of reference if one wishes to speak theologically about humanity and the Church's important witness in the last century. There is nothing truly human that does not resonate in the heart of the disciples of Christ, because nothing truly human failed to find an echo in the heart of the Lord. The primacy of humanity, even over the sabbath and the Law, is to be found at the heart of the Gospel. In this sense, the Christian view of humanity may be considered a type of humanism, as it proposes humanity to be the center of the world. It also says that the human being is the only creature in this world who God has loved in and of itself[43].

But there is also a radical difference: if humanism proclaims that we are the measure of all things, Christianity proclaims that there is another measure for humanity: Jesus. This is a measure we have not given to ourselves, because the incarnate Son of God is the great gift of God that came to us through the free

---

40 *Gaudium et Spes* 12: «Believers and non-believers are, generally, in agreement with this point: all the earth's bounties ought to be ordered on behalf of man, center and peak of all of them». Cfr. also JOHN PAUL II, *Fides et Ratio* 67: «In studying revelation and its credibility, as well as the corresponding act of faith, fundamental theology should show how, in the light of the knowledge conferred by faith, there emerge certain truths which reason, from its own independent enquiry, already perceives. Revelation endows these truths with their fullest meaning, directing them towards the richness of the revealed mystery in which they find their ultimate purpose».

41 Cfr. JOHN PAUL II, *Veritatis Splendor* 16.

42 Cfr. *Gaudium et Spes* 1-22.

43 Cfr. *Gaudium et Spes* 24.

initiative of the Father. It is the measure God has given us so that we may attain our own perfection. But it is a measure that is neither alien nor exterior to us. It is the measure of the one who lived in communion with his fellow human beings most radically —the unblemished Lamb who died for the sins of others. With no other human being may we be as close as we are with him, who lives in us more deeply than we live ourselves (cfr. Gal 2:20). Otherwise, the measure of humanity is the one that is the image of the Father (cfr. Col 1:15; 2 Cor 4:4), the God whom no one has seen but who has been made known to us by the firstborn (cfr. John 1:18). Jesus directs us to God, and it is only through him that we come to know what our ultimate criterion for our humanity should be. Christian revelation has been given soundness, and has filled with meaning the affirmation found in Genesis: «in the image of God he created them, male and female he created them» (Gen 1:27).

The creaturely image of God, called to participate in his life, is the paradox of the human being, who cannot attain his fullness except in that which radically surpasses it, and who is frustrated to the extent that he stays locked into his own possibilities and horizons. There is no other possible perfection except the one that may take him beyond his limits, and therefore the one he can only freely receive as a gift from God. Human beings are unable to attain the fullness of our being by ourselves. We must abandon ourselves to God and must trust in him. The human being must open himself up to hope, and «he who claims what is due him does not wait; because if I am owed something, I demand it as a right»[44]. This is the paradox of the human being spoken of by H. de Lubac[45]. The deepest part about ourselves is pure gift. As creatures of God, our very existence is a gift, and the call to divine Sonship in Christ, which in the end determines our personal identity, is a gift as well. We did not «exist» before God called us to communion with him, and our personal being is, indeed, called to communion with God and to share in the mission of Christ.[46] The most intimate reality about us is what

---

44 HILARY OF POITIERS, *Tr. Ps.* 15,4 (PL 9,893).

45 DE LUBAC H., *Le mystère du surnaturel*, Paris 1965, 209: «If it is true that this vision of God, in essence, is our effective destiny, and hence, is the God towards which, one or another way, is the inclination of our nature; how can it be for nothing? A second antonym, added to the first: we are creatures, and we have been promised the vision of God. The desire to see him is in us. It is in ourselves, and even so it is fulfilled only by a gift».

46 On this point, the reflections of DE LUBAC H. are also essential, ibid., 105-109. He cites an interesting text from SAINT AUGUSTINE, *Conf.* I 20,1: «Ista omnia Dei mei dona sunt, et bona sunt, et haec omnia ego».

is least our own, and again the Christological reference becomes necessary: the personal being of Christ, the Son of God, is constituted by his relationship with the Father and the Holy Spirit.

In our condition as creatures and human persons, we are not in pure relationship with God and with others. This is demonstrated, in other ways, by the fact that we can shut ourselves off from the love of God and others. There is in us an inevitable tension between self-centering and opening ourselves to others. But this does not mean that the path taking us to full realization of what we are is unclear. Our personal being, insofar as we are called to divine sonship in the first-begotten Son, finds its fullness only in the free giving of ourselves to God and others. The dimensions of *sonship* and *brotherhood*, as we know, are inseparable. The Spirit of God and of Christ, the gift of the Risen One, is what makes possible our total giving to God and to others. This liberates us from ourselves in the freedom of the children of God. The Spirit is the beginning of our response to the divine call. He also guided Jesus in his historical and human path to the Father. In the Spirit of Christ, we may call God «Father» (cfr. Rom 8:15; Gal 4: 6). Our life of sonship in the Spirit means the fullness of our personal being, by conforming ourselves to Jesus, who, in the total exercise of his freedom, as a human being, delivered himself unto death for our sake.

The perfection of human nature is found solely in that which surpasses it. The fathers of the Church intimated this, understanding that without the Spirit of God, the divine and transcendent reality, human beings could never fully become themselves. Thus writes Saint Irenaeus of Lyons: «He calls perfect those who have received the Spirit of God … This Spirit —blended with the soul— joins the body, and brings about, thanks to the coming of the Spirit, the spiritual and perfect man. Such is man created in the image and likeness of God (cfr. Gen 1:26)»[47]. And somewhat later he adds: «As we have stated, there are three elements in the perfect man: flesh, soul and spirit. The one, the spirit, saves and conforms; the other, flesh, is united and conformed; while the soul, between them, when it follows the Spirit is raised by him, and when it gives into flesh it succumbs to earthly concupiscence»[48]. Our interest at this point is not in citing all other passages like this one[49]. Our interest is to underscore two elements: on the

---

47 IRENAEUS OF LYONS, *Adv. Haer.* v 6,1.

48 IRENAEUS OF LYONS, *Adv. Haer.* Ibid., v 9,1. For an exhaustive commentary of these texts, see ORBE A., *Teología de San Ireneo* I, Madrid-Toledo 1985, 291-297, 406-415.

49 On the meaning of this distinction, see CCE 367, where it points out that the «spirit» in this context signifies the ordering of man to the divine realm from the moment of his creation, thus

one hand, the newness of Christian anthropology, which, while accepting the philosophical notion of humanity as consisting of body and soul, is not satisfied with it, because the divine element, which is pure gift, is not explicit, and while its transcendence is not in any way ignored, it comes to constitute the perfect man (Saint Augustine uses the phrase *interior intimo meo* in another key passage with a similar fundamental concern). Only the Spirit may take humanity beyond itself to the glory of resurrection in the likeness of Christ.

On the other hand, there is the matter of human responsibility and freedom, gifts of God that enable us to tend toward either the sublime or the terrestrial, the spiritual or the flesh. It is otherwise obvious that this second choice does not properly free humanity, but rather makes us fall back into the slavery of sin and passions. Only by accepting life in the Spirit are we placed on the path of real freedom. Saint Irenaeus shows us clearly the true meaning of human freedom: it is above all the capacity to accept or reject God's gift given to us in Christ. In every exercise that humans make with their freedom, we more or less move within the range of this last horizon of our responsibility before God. This is the capacity for human self-determination, which places man in the sequence of concrete options. A new sense of freedom thus appears, and human responsibilities are explained in terms of their own dimension and of transcendent destiny. The human being is free, first and foremost, before God, and it is before him that he must answer for his actions and omissions.

A New Vision of Humanity

There is no doubt that Christianity centers its concern in the human person while defending its unique value over everything around us. This has many common elements with diverse anthropological perspectives that share an interest in humanity and the defense of its dignity and rights. A broad margin of cooperation —on many levels— opens up this domain for Christians, including with those who do not share our faith. But the knowledge of Christ, the incarnate Son of God,

Chapter 2

63

---

pertaining to the capacity of his soul and of the free elevation of it to God. It then becomes obvious that this is not a purely anthropological dimension, but one of the divine vocation of humanity, which is not the case after his creation, and, for reasons already mentioned, is a structural element in the identity of each human being.

offers us a vision of humanity that opens up a new horizon of great value in other worldviews, and which demonstrates what we have been able to discover through our own efforts. This demonstrates, above all, the essential relationship every human person has with God, not just because he created us, but because we have been created in his image and likeness, called to be a son or daughter in Jesus, the perfect image of the Father, and to participate in the glory of his resurrection. The incarnation of the Son confers upon humanity its highest dignity. Through it, Jesus united himself with every one of us, especially the poor and little ones. Hence, humanity achieves the fundamental dignity which it deserves. Every human person —and the whole of humanity— are thus called to be *children of God* and the *temple of the Holy Spirit*. We become *sons* and *daughters* of God, and *brothers* and *sisters* in Christ, who is not ashamed to call us as such (cfr. Heb 2:11-12), in *a brotherhood devoid of frontiers under the fatherhood of God.*

64   Christians know that everything we have is a pure gift of God, which we can accept only in gratitude and trust. At the same time, we are aware that we are responsible for our own actions, and in some measure those of our neighbor. We are free to open ourselves to the grace of God as well as to shut ourselves off from it, even if doing so paradoxically destroys our freedom. We know our life is saved only if we surrender it. We know, too, that we will never truly become who we were meant to be, except by giving of ourselves to others, allowing the Spirit to guide us toward our rightful destiny. But all of this does not make Christians slaves of an external force that depersonalizes them; rather, only in this way can Christians live in true freedom as the children of God. Christians have a clear and precise point of reference in Jesus, the perfect man who, in obedience to the Father, handed over his life, died for our sins, and rose for our justification (cfr. Rom 4:25). Jesus himself invites us to take up our cross and follow him in order to share in his glory. A person, not an idea, is the center of Christian anthropology. This is its most radical and definitive newness. Ignatius of Antioch had an unsurpassable intuition when, facing imminent martyrdom, he became aware that conformity with Jesus in his death is the highest realization of humanity. Ignatius' words may be used as both a summary and conclusion for our reflection: «I look for him who died for us. I love him who is risen for us ... Don't stop his living; don't wish his death ... Allow me to attain pure light. When this happens I will be a man. Allow me to be imitator of the passion of my God»[50].

50 IGNATIUS OF ANTIOCH, *To the Romans* 6,1,3 (FP 1,154-157).

Christ's Salvation and the Salvation of All

1

Salvation: God, Humanity, and Encounter

When we consider the theme of salvation from the point of view of Christian faith and theology, two perspectives necessarily confront each other: that of humanity, fragile and full of need, which necessarily thinks about its own good and fulfillment and which does not in itself have all we would want, and that of the gift of God, which Christ brings to us[1]. The latter necessarily incorporates a reference to the concrete situation of humanity. Otherwise it would be a difficult language, not to say impossible, to understand. The term salvation elicits interest in us because we feel the need for it. We all desire liberation from the negative aspects of our lives; in any case, we have always before us the disturbing horizon of death. At the same time, our longing for salvation purports the desire for fulfillment of the good things we enjoy, of the positive aspects of our existence, which we acknowledge as such, but always see as flawed by the inherent imperfection of the human condition. On the other hand, it is not obvious that all human beings think in the same way about salvation. The diversity of anthropological notions necessarily implies diverse ideas about human fulfillment. We cannot understand independently what we think of ourselves, where we come from and where we are going, and what the meaning of our freedom and our responsibility is. If we could align our questioning concerning the negative aspects of our lives that we would wish to see eliminated, an agreement on the positive contents we wish to attain might be a difficult one to reach. The words of the Second Vatican Council are interesting:

> As a creature he experiences his limitations in a multitude of ways; on the other hand he
> feels himself to be boundless in his desires and summoned to a higher life… Indeed,
> as a weak and sinful being, he often does what he would not, and fails to do what he
> would. Hence he suffers from internal divisions, and from these flow so many and
> such great discords in society. No doubt many whose lives are infected with a practical
> materialism are blinded against any sharp insight into this kind of dramatic situation;
> or else, weighed down by unhappiness, they are prevented from giving the matter any

1 Cfr. LADARIA L.F., «Salvezza di Cristo e salvezza dell'uomo» in *Archivio Teologico Torinese* 11 (2005) 35-52; LADARIA L.F., «El cristianismo, oferta de salvación» published in *La transmisión de la fe: la propuesta cristiana en la era secular.* VI Jornadas de Teología, Santiago de Compostela 2005, 171-195.

thought. Thinking they have found serenity in an interpretation of reality everywhere proposed these days, many look forward to a genuine and total emancipation of humanity wrought solely by human effort; they are convinced that the future rule of man over the earth will satisfy every desire of his heart… Nevertheless, in the face of the modern development of the world, the number constantly swells of the people who raise the most basic questions or recognize them with a new sharpness: what is man? What is this sense of sorrow, of evil, of death, which continues to exist despite so much progress? What purpose have these victories purchased at so high a cost? What can man offer to society, and what can he expect from it? What follows this earthly life?[2].

This plurality of conceptions and visions of humanity is accompanied very frequently by the failures of the attempts to reach completion through our own efforts alone. The answer of the Council to these questions is proposed from the perspective of Christian faith. «Christ, who died and was raised up for all», the only Savior, gives humanity the possibility of responding to their vocation. In him we find «the key, the focal point and the goal of man, as well as of all human history»[3].

It is understandable that even from the beginning *Gaudium et Spes*, mindful of the problems of humanity, should place humankind in the light of Christ. This is because, if on the one hand, it is necessary that we face the problem of salvation, keeping in mind our weakness and indigence, then on the other hand, we must not forget that when we encounter Christ the expectations of the heart

2   *Gaudium et Spes* 10. After some years, the *International Theological Commission* offers a diagnosis with other nuances: «What is found is a cultural and intellectual pluralism, a broad range of different analyses of the human condition and a variety of paths to attempt to face them. Next to a sort of escape into a pleasant enjoyment or the absorbing and transitory attractions of hedonism, is a return to various ideologies and mythologies. Together with a somewhat resigned, lucid and valiant Stoicism, there are both a disillusion pretending to be realist and tenacious and a resolute protest against the reduction of human beings and their milieu to market resources to be exploited … In the contemporary situation, therefore, a fact is clear enough: *the concrete situation of human beings is full of ambiguities*… For example, in each individual, there is, on the one hand, a desire for life, impossible to eradicate, and on the other hand, the experience of the limit, of non-satisfaction, of failure and of suffering. Going from the individual sphere to the general, the same picture can be seen on a broader fabric. Also here, on one hand, the huge progress by science and technology can be pointed out by the mass media and by advances reached —for example— in the field of private, public and international law. On the other hand, there are so many catastrophes in the world, and between peoples, so much deprivation, resulting in very large numbers of people who suffer terrible oppression and exploitation and who become defenseless victims of what in fact may appear to be only their cruel fate». COMISIÓN TEOLÓGICA INTERNACIONAL, *Documentos 1969-1996*, POZO C., S.J. (ed.) BAC, Madrid 1998, 508-509.
3   *Gaudium et Spes* 10.

are indeed exceeded, but also, very frequently, turned upside down. We cannot think of a human desire that is simply satisfied. Only in the encounter with Christ can we see clearly the meaning of the salvation he is bringing us. The episode of Paul at the Areopagus in Athens is significant: if he presented himself announcing the unknown God whom the Greeks had somehow glimpsed, when he began to speak of a central and specific point of the Christian message of salvation, namely, the resurrection of the dead, his word encountered rejection (cfr. Acts 17:22-23). There cannot be an encounter with Christ without conversion. We find this in the first words of the teaching of Jesus that the Gospel of Mark transmits: «The time is fulfilled, and the kingdom of God has come near; repent, and believe the good news» (Mark 1:15; cfr. Matt 3:17). To welcome the Kingdom, the object of the hope of Israel, to welcome what is defined from the start as good news, conversion is needed. Is there not something paradoxical to this idea? We need conversion for the good news to clearly appear as such. We have to change our minds to be able to receive what saves us. The paradox is illuminated if we keep in mind that in the mystery of our salvation we have to encounter God, who gives himself to us in total freedom, this God that, as much as we grow, is always much larger, as Saint Augustine has reminded us[4].

The salvation God offers us goes beyond our expectations. It is not the one we want to receive, but rather the one he wants to give us. The International Theological Commission expressed the idea in these terms:

> Redemption refers to God —as the author of our redemption— before it refers to us, and only because it is thus can redemption truly signify liberation for us and be the Good News of salvation for all the time and for all times. This means that only because redemption primarily refers to the glorious bounty of God rather than to our need —although redemption deals with that necessity— it is a liberating reality for us. If, on the other hand, redemption *had* to be judged or measured by the existential need of human beings, how could we avoid the suspicion of having simply created a Redeemer God in the image of our own need?[5]

---

4 AUGUSTINE, *En in Ps.* 62,16 (CCL 39,804): «Semper enim ille maior est, quantumque creverimus». The greater nearness of God always makes him appear larger.

5 COMISIÓN TEOLÓGICA INTERNACIONAL, *Documentos 1969-1996*, POZO C., S.J. (ed.) BAC, Madrid 1998, 500.

It is God himself who, when we deal with the offer of Christian salvation made present in Christ, places himself at the center. It is he who has to be welcomed and accepted with the same freedom with which he gives himself to us. We cannot make him the mechanism of anything, not even of our transcendent salvation, because as a consequence we would not allow him to be God, and therefore, we would remain enclosed within our own limitations. We approach God because he approaches us, we know him because he previously knows us, we can follow him because he shows us how to do so, and we look for him because he has already placed in the depths of our heart the desire to find him[6]. This first «descending» moment in the encounter with God makes itself present even in the knowledge we may have of him from creation. God, through everything he has created, offers humanity a perennial witnessing of himself, as the Second Vatican Council teaches us (*Dei Verbum* 3; cfr. Rom 1:19-20). This testimony has to be welcomed, with all the more reason since his salvation is intrinsically bound to him, as we will see in our exposition. Pauline teachings on justification by faith are a perpetual reminder and an admonition of this absolute primacy of God himself. It is a matter of receiving, and even more, of letting God receive us, of letting us be reconciled with him (cfr. 2 Cor 5:18-20), of letting us be consoled by God so that we are able to console those who find themselves in great tribulation (cfr. 2 Cor 1:3-4).

On the other hand, to consider this divine initiative is to contemplate it in a design embracing the whole of history, established before the existence of the world, a design that has Christ at its center and that has not yet reached its completion: «Blessed *be* the God and Father of our Lord Jesus Christ, who has blessed us with every spiritual blessing in the heavenly *places,* just as he has chosen us in Christ before the foundation of the world… He has made known to us the mystery of his will, according to his good pleasure that he set forth in Christ, as a plan for the fullness of time to gather up all things in him, things in heaven, and

---

6 ANSELM OF CANTERBURY, *Proslogion I. Opera* I 98: «Domine Deus meus, doce cor meum ubi et quomodo te quaerat, ubi et quomodo te inveniat». *Opera* I 100: «Doce me quaerere Te, et ostende Te quaerenti; quia nec quaerere Te possum nisi Tu doceas, nec inveniri nisi Te ostendas… Fateor Domine, et gratias ago, quia creasti me in hanc imaginem tuam, ut tui memor Te cogitem». *Opere* I 14,384: «Aut potuit [quis] omnino aliquid intelligere de Te, nisi per lucem tuam et veritatem tuam?». SAINT BERNARD, *Liber de diligendo Deo* VII (PL 182,987): «Nemo quarere te valet, nisi qui prius invenerit. Potes quidam quaeri et inveniri, non tamen praeveniri». Cfr. CABADA CASTRO M., *El Dios que da que pensar. Acceso filosófico-antropológico a la divinidad,* BAC, Madrid 1999, 384; GONZÁLEZ DE CARDEDAL O., *Dios,* Sígueme, Salamanca 2004², 104-105; AMENGUAL G., *La religió en temps de nihilisme,* Cruilla, Barcelona 2004, 108-109.

things on earth» (Eph 1:3-4, 9-10). It is not only that God is first in the plan of salvation, and that what we must first keep in mind is his goodness toward us which is freely manifested. The salvation of humanity, however, affects not only each and every one of us, but also involves the realization of God's cosmic design to be brought about in his Son, Jesus Christ — a project that began with creation and that is to be fulfilled in the *parousia*. The recapitulation of everything in Christ is the objective of the whole divine action *ad extra*. Christ must destroy all principalities, domains, and powers, and he must reign until he has subjected all his enemies at his feet (cfr. Ps 110:1; Heb 10:13), so that he may then deliver the kingdom to the Father and submit to him[7], so that God may be all in all (cfr. 1 Cor 15:4-28). The reference to God before ourselves justifies the need to come out of ourselves and our own categories and schemes so that we may enter God's orbit that Christ reveals to us.

Added to this is another fundamental reason, one that the Gospel references more directly concerning the need for conversion. Christian salvation is, in one of its fundamental dimensions, but clearly not the only one, liberation from sin. Even without sin, humans would always be weak and impoverished beings before God, and thus in need of salvation. But the tragedy of sin shouldered by humanity from the beginning of time underscores the need for conversion and for welcoming the Good News. Christian salvation has a component of liberation and redemption[8]. This fact highlights the need to accept and welcome salvation that comes to us from God. This is another demonstration of the impossibility of salvation through our own means. We cannot do so, among other reasons, because liberation from sin and from our old humanity means liberation from ourselves[9]. In order to reach that which we are called to be, we have to be liberated from the heavy load that impedes our journey. Paradoxically, we will never be able to grasp it in its totality; only as salvation draws closer to us will we

---

7 Submission opens an ecclesiological theme of major significance. In the theology of the early Church fathers, the submission of Christ is not so much a personal one, since he has always fulfilled the will of the Father, but rather that of the group of those saved, which brings about the fulfillment of the Body of Christ.

8 SESBOÜÉ B., *Jésus-Christ l'unique mediateur. Essai sur la rédemption et le salut,* Paris 2003², 27: «In the language of Scriptures and of ecclesial tradition we find both of these aspects of our salvation: liberation from sin and divinization. If the West has better underscored the redeeming side properly, the East has enjoyed more the highlighting of the divinizing side. But to distinguish is not to separate. It is obvious that both of these dimensions, whichever be underscored, constitute a concrete unity which ought to be always respected».

9 Cfr. DE LUBAC H., *Petite chatéchèse sur Nature et Grâce,* Paris 1980, 113: «For his salvation man has to be liberated from his sin, liberated from himself».

be able to grasp the depths of our sin. «Go away from me, Lord, for I am a sinful man» is the spontaneous reaction of Peter after the first miraculous catch of fish (cfr. Luke 5:8; Isa 6:5). The nearness of God, and in particular, of Christ, in whom God manifests himself in a definitive way, makes us more aware of our degradation, and thus of our need to be saved. Only in the light of Christ does our sin, in all of its gravity, come before our eyes; only through him can we become aware of the God whose love we have rejected[10]. Salvation, a total gift from God, requires the acceptance and cooperation of humanity. Hence, it requires our conversion, since we have moved away from God: «This saying is sure, and worthy of full acceptance, that Christ Jesus came into the world to save sinners —of whom I am the foremost» (1Tim 1:15). And all human beings are sinners: «All have sinned and lack God's glory» (Rom 3:23). Without going into «hamartiocentrism», which sees human sin as the unleashing of the saving mechanism of God's love, we cannot forget the part that human sin has played in the cross of Christ[11], who did not know sin but was been made sin by us so that in him we might be the righteousness of God (cfr. 2 Cor 5:19-21), he who on the wood of the cross bore our sins so that we might live for righteousness (1 Pet 2: 22-24).

The good news is only for those who let themselves be shaped by it, that is, those who believe and accept in freedom the salvation God offers us in Christ. This idea clearly appears in the farewell address of Jesus in the Gospel of Mark: «And he said unto them, Go into all the world, and preach the gospel to every creature. He who believes and is baptized shall be saved; but he who does not believe shall be condemned» (Mark 16:15-16). The good news, and the invitation to receive it in faith, has as its object the salvation of humanity. And one of the first statements of faith we find in the New Testament securely binds the acceptance of the message of the lordship of Christ and his resurrection from the dead with the salvation of whoever welcomes and confesses it: «That if you confess

10 GONZÁLEZ DE CARDEDAL O., *Cristología*, BAC, Madrid 2001, 551: «The sin of Adam is discovered since Christ, our guilt since the forgiveness God offers us, and our omitted responsibilities in the light of the Spirit. The world in sin is, indeed, the one calling itself just, the one that claims being exempted from guilt. And this one is the supreme sin (John 9:39-41; 15:22). In this sense, the discovery of sin is a fruit of redemption». Cfr. LADARIA L.F., *Teología del pecado original y de la gracia,* BAC, Madrid 2004⁴, 109: «In the revelation of Jesus it is clear which is the love rejected by human beings. Whoever knows Christ and accepts salvation which comes from him becomes aware of the perdition of life without Christ».

11 ANSELM OF CANTERBURY, *Cur Deus homo* I 21 (*Opera* II 88), speaks of the «weight of sin» (*pondus peccati*), which makes redemption necessary. We can only understand this weight in its just measure if we consider the love of God that sin has rejected.

with your lips that Jesus is Lord, and believe in your heart that God raised him from the dead, you will be saved. For one believes with the heart and so is justified; and one confesses with the mouth and so is saved» (Rom 10:9-10). Salvation comes, ultimately, from the love of God, who gives his only Son to the world, so that whoever believes in him may have eternal life, and he sends his Son not to condemn the world but for it to be saved through him (cfr. John 3:16-17). And «God proves his love for us in that while we were still sinners Christ died for us. Much more surely, now that we have been justified by his blood, we will be saved through him from the wrath of God. For if, while we were enemies, we were reconciled to God through the death of his Son, much more surely, having been reconciled, we will be saved by his life» (Rom 5:8-10). The New Testament, like the Old, cannot be understood without the offer of salvation made by God to humanity in a unique design of love that begins with creation and reaches its culmination in Christ.

In our encounter with the Lord, we are invited to look to him, toward the realization of his work, of God's design to recapitulate «all things in him, things in heaven and things on earth» (Eph 1:10). Our salvation takes place in the realm of a project in which God himself has become engaged and before which he is not indifferent. Christ must destroy all principalities, dominions, and powers, and must reign until he subdues his enemies; once everything has submitted to him, he will submit to the one to whom everything has submitted, so that God may be all in all (cfr. 1 Cor 15:14-28; Eph 1:13; Ps 110:1). This project of God is still in the stage of realization. The work of Christ has not yet been fully realized, and everyone's salvation can take place only in the realm of that design which embraces the whole of humanity. «God our Savior… who desires everyone to be saved and to come to the knowledge of the truth» (1 Tim 2:3-4). To work out this salvation, God has sent his Son into the world. Human salvation is, therefore, the realization of the Father's plan and the victory of Christ over the enemy.

The reflections of Hans Urs von Balthasar regarding the possibility of humanity's damnation are pertinent precisely because they contemplate the salvation of humanity within God's work as well as Christ's victory: while *gloria Dei* remained assured in any case, in the case of salvation, as well as in the case of damnation, the problem was not an acute one. But when the finality of creation is intimately connected to the Trinitarian life, this question becomes unavoidable[12].

---

12 Cfr. VON BALTHASAR H.U., *Teodramática 5. El último acto*, Madrid 1997, 490 (the German original was published in 1983); *Kleiner Diskurs über die Hölle,* Ostfildern 1987.

Of course, it is not a matter of returning to the theses of the *apokatastasis*, which are incompatible with the Christian message insofar as, among other things, they empty salvation of meaning: if human freedom is not considered, and with it the possibility of rejecting the divine offer, then salvation becomes something forced; it is no longer the free answer to love that love calls for. But, indeed, it should be maintained that God is not indifferent before the dual possibility of our salvation or damnation; according to our human way of reasoning, our possible rejection of his invitation means that his plan of salvation is not completely realized.

Karl Rahner, too, insisted on the fact that Christian eschatology be, above all, a message of salvation, and one that must not be reduced to a neutral discussion. The eschatology of salvation and the eschatology of damnation are not found at the same level. There is only one predestination —that of salvation in Christ— and eschatology is, from this point of view, the affirmation of the grace of Christ, who conquered and perfected the world. Naturally, for reasons already stated, no one can know for sure in this life, if she/he will be included in or excluded from Christ's victory[13]. The realization of Christ's work and human salvation are intimately connected.

2

Salvation in Christ

The texts we have previously cited clearly hint at an aspect that some passages in the New Testament will express more explicitly, namely, that this offer of salvation is not primordially linked to a message, not even to a statement of faith in set truths. Rather, in a more radical fashion, it is tied to someone who is the base and origin of all these things: the very person of Jesus: «The stone that the builders rejected has become the chief cornerstone» (Ps 118:22). «For there is no other name under heaven given among mortals by which we must be saved» (Acts 4:11-12). This is certainly an unprecedented statement, which after twenty centuries of Christianity continues to create difficulties and even scandal: how can the salvation of all humanity be attributed to one man, whom the great majority of

---

13 Cfr. RAHNER K., «Principios de la hermenéutica de las declaraciones escatológicas» in *Escritos de teología* IV, Madrid 1964, 411-439, 431-432.

human beings have not known and perhaps will never know? Should not the Church give up this pretension of seeing Christ as the sole savior of all of humanity? In doing so, would not the Church grow in credibility in the eyes of its contemporaries? These questions notwithstanding, New Testament statements do not allow for any doubt (cfr. 1 Tim 2:3-6; John 1:29; 14:6; 1 John 4:14; 2 Cor 5:19). The Church feels linked to these statements, the Church of today as well as the Church of all times[14]. The Christian offer of salvation cannot be other than that of Christ, who has come so that all may have life and may have it in abundance (cfr. John 10:10) and has given his life in ransom for all (cfr. Matt 20:28; Mark 10:45).

The name of Jesus indicates that his saving mission is essential to understand his coming into the world: «She will bear a son, and you are to name him Jesus: for he will save his people from their sins» (Matt 1:21). It is God's salvation that makes itself present in Jesus. From the first moment of his existence on earth, Jesus appears as the envoy of God sent to free humanity from sin. Salvation is, from the very beginning, essentially linked to his person. The path of salvation necessarily leads to the Savior; furthermore, it will be this same person who will give meaning and determine the contents of salvation itself. In fact, in Christ a new possibility of fulfillment and new life is offered to us, which, begun in this life, will find, in the new heavens and the new earth announced by the prophets and begun in the resurrection of Christ, its definitive fullness.

The texts we've previously cited invite us to take this step, which in the New Testament is made more explicit when it attributes the title of «Savior» to Jesus. This title might have generated some uneasiness at the beginning, but it appears in the pastoral letters and in 2 Peter, frequently applied both to Christ and to God[15] (applied to Christ: Luke 2:11; John 4:42; Heb 5:31; 13:23; Eph 5:23; Phil 3:30;

---

14 CONGREGATION FOR THE DOCTRINE OF THE FAITH, declaration *Dominus Iesus* on the unicity and salvific universality of Jesus Christ and the Church, Vatican, Rome 2000. Cfr. some teaching texts: DH 624; 1522; 1523; 2005.

15 This title might have caused problems early on, as it might have had Hellenic echoes. Cfr. PONTIFICIAL BIBLICAL COMMISSION, *The Jewish People and their Sacred Scriptures in the Christian Bible, 32* (Published by Libreria Editrice Vaticana, Città del Vaticano 2001): «It can be said that in the Gospels, the Acts of the Apostles and in the uncontested Pauline Letters, the New Testament is very sparing in its use of the title Saviour. This reticence is explained by the fact that the title was widely used in the Hellenistic world; it was conferred on gods such as Asclepius, a healer god, and on divinized kings who were hailed as saviors of the people. The title, then, could become ambiguous. Furthermore, the notion of salvation in the Greek world had a strong individual and physical connotation, while the New Testament, in continuity with the Old, had collective amplitude and was open to the spiritual. With the passage of time, the danger of ambiguity lessened. The Pastoral Letters and Second Peter use the title Saviour often and apply it both to God and to Christ».

2 Tim 1:10; Titus 1:4; 2:13; 3:6; 2 Pet 1:1.11; 2:20; 3:2.18; 1 John 4:14; applied to God: Luke 1:47; 1 Tim 1:1; 2:3; 4:10; Titus 1:3; 2:10; 3:4; Jude 25). The fact that Jesus can be considered the «Savior», as well as the Father, has a profound meaning for salvation. This fact demonstrates that the salvation which Jesus brings us does not come, in a manner of speaking, solely on his initiative; ultimately, it comes from God. It should be noted that in most cases where the title is given to God, Christ is not outside the biblical perspective (cfr. 1 Tim 1:1; 2:3-6; Titus 1:3-4; 2:10; 13; 3:4-6; Jude 25), so that it is clear that this salvation which comes to us from God, who wants all of us to be saved and who is also called «savior of all» (1 Tim 4:10), is not realized without the work of the sole mediator, the man Christ Jesus (cfr. Tim 2:3-6). There is no salvation from God except the one that takes place in Christ. This fact essentially determines salvation itself, both in its manner of realization and in its content. Savior and salvation cannot be separated. The salvation that comes to us by the mediation of Christ is clothed in unusual and unrepeatable characteristics: Christ has not limited himself to putting God and humanity in contact and to bringing about the recovery of friendship between the two without being deeply affected by this fact. Albert Vanhoye says: «Christ has not been content with only doing an external work of mediation, but he has realized that mediation in his own person»[16]. We must reflect on the ways in which the person of Christ enters into the mediation between God and humanity and thus determines salvation for the latter. It will help us to look into the articulation of some of the dimensions of salvation as the work of God and Christ.

3
Christ's «Perfection»: Origin of our Salvation

We may continue our reflection by looking at a fundamental passage of the letter to the Hebrews, which speaks about Christ's petition to spare him from death, and that in spite of his divine condition, he learned or experienced obedience, thus attaining perfection:

---

16 VANHOYE A., *La Lettre aux Hébreux. Jésus-Christ médiateur d'une nouvelle alliance*, Paris 2002, 103.

In the days of his flesh, Jesus offered up prayers and supplications, with loud cries and tears, to the one who was able to save him from death, and he was heard because of his reverent submission. Although he was a Son, he learned obedience through what he suffered; and having been made perfect, he became the source of eternal salvation for all who obey him; having been designated by God a high priest according to the order of Melchizedek (Heb 5:7-10).

Jesus, the Son of God, in the perfection obtained in his humanity through obedience, is the cause of eternal salvation for all who obey him[17]. It is worthwhile to reflect a little on the relationship between this perfection of Jesus and our salvation. The beseeching prayer of Jesus shows us his participation in human weakness, having been tested in everything like us, yet without sin (Heb 4:15). This participation opens up for us the deep mystery of Christ, who knows himself to be in perfect communion with the Father and participating in his power (cfr. John 5:19-36; 11:41-42). This is the first aspect of the mediation in his very person that we mentioned. But there is more. In his prayer he listens in an attitude of reverence; this begins in his internal transformation: in suffering he learned obedience, and because of this he has reached perfection and has been able to become the cause of eternal salvation for all who believe in him. Naturally, such learning was not personally needed because he was the Son since the beginning (cfr. Heb 4:14; 5:8). But it was convenient for his mediator function once the incarnation had taken place, and the demands of redemption are taken seriously until the end. From the moment Jesus entered the world he was in a disposition of submission, but this is not the same thing as going through an actual ordeal:

> Only thanks to the painful test does the original disposition penetrate all fibers in human nature. If in the test, the disposition of loving docility towards God is maintained, a positive transformation is obtained by the test. Already one is not the same; one is bonded to God in a stronger and deeper manner. It is this type of transformation which has taken place in the human nature of Christ, which has allowed him to move from earthly fragility to divine perfection[18].

---

17 Cfr. VANHOYE A., *La Lettre aux Hébreux*, 103-104, for what follows.
18 VANHOYE A., *La Lettre aux Hébreux*, 105.

78

By virtue of this perfection, which is the cause of salvation of all, there are two intimately related elements. Perfection is both the perfection of humanity and that of the mediator; they are entwined[19]. It could be said that the perfection of Christ and the salvation of humanity are two inseparable faces of the same coin. In the light of this priestly theology of the letter to the Hebrews, Jesus' condition of being savior as well as God himself, who does not exercise this condition without Christ's mediation, acquires some very precise connotations. Through the actions of the Father as well as his own obedience, Christ, as a man, attains the perfection of union with God and the perfection of union with humanity in the most complete solidarity[20].

If this text in the letter to the Hebrews is especially significant, it is not the only one in which human salvation is related to the fullness of the humanity of Christ. Other places present more explicitly the resurrection and glorification of Christ.

According to John 17:5, Jesus asks the Father to be glorified with the glory he enjoyed, together with the Father, before the world came into being. And this glory is that which the disciples should contemplate: the glory Jesus has because the Father loved him before the creation of the world, and whose contemplation shall gives us fullness: «Father, I desire that those also, whom you have given me to be with me where I am, to see my glory which you have given me because you loved me before the foundation of the world» (John 17:24). Jesus is the Son of God from the first moment of his incarnation (cfr. Luke 1:35); furthermore, he existed as the Son and as God next to the Father before he came to the world to save us (cfr. John 1:1-2; 3:6-17; Rom 8:3; Gal 4:4). But having divested himself of the form of God and dwelling among us as a slave, in obedience unto death on the cross, he needed to be exalted by the Father (cfr. Phil 2:2-11), to be glorified by him and recover the glory he possessed before time began. As a human, being tested as we are in everything, yet without sin (cfr. Heb 4:15), Jesus reached perfection and has been saved from death: «For you do not give me up to *Sheol* or let your faithful one see the Pit» (Ps 16:10; Acts 2:27; 2:29-32).

Jesus, therefore, has been saved and liberated by the Father, and his divine Sonship, possessed before the beginning of time, has been perfected in regard to his humanity. Only thus can he save those who obey him. Through the resurrection Jesus is constituted as the Son of God (cfr. Rom 1:3-4), Lord of all (cfr. Phil

19 Cfr. VANHOYE A., *La Lettre aux Hébreux*, 106.
20 Cfr. VANHOYE A., *La Lettre aux Hébreux*, 108.

2:11), and, ascended to heaven, he sits at the right hand of the Father (cfr. Mark 16:19; Acts 2:34). The resurrection itself is interpreted in the New Testament in terms of «generation», that is, in the fullness of divine Sonship (cfr. Acts 13:33; Ps 2:7; Heb 1:5; 5:5). The salvation of humanity is in intrinsic relationship with the fullness of Christ's humanity in the resurrection. He, who by dying has conquered death, gives us the possibility of being conformed in accordance with his glorious body, so that we may bear the image of the celestial Adam, the risen Jesus, after having borne that of the earthly Adam (cfr. 1 Cor 15:45-49). God has predestined us to reproduce the image of his Son so that he may be firstborn among many (cfr. Rom 8:29). The salvation of humanity cannot be separated from the fullness of Christ; it can only participate in it (cfr. John 1:16).

The relationship between the fullness of Christ by the work of the Father and that of his humanity, which is already present in the New Testament, has been also an object of explicit reflection in patristic theology. Justin Martyr, for example, had to face the question of the meaning of the human history of Jesus in his *Dialogue with Tryphon*. Two moments in the life of Christ acquire special significance in this sense: in the first place, the baptism in the Jordan with the coming of the Holy Spirit upon him, and in the second place, the resurrection. We must bear in mind an element that joins these two moments in an essential relationship: the reference to the divine Sonship of Jesus (cfr. Mark 1:11; Acts 13:33; Rom 1:4)[21].

Let us go to the first of these mysteries in the life of Christ. Tryphon, a Jew, asks Justin if Jesus is the pre-existing Son of God, then what possible meaning can the descent of the Holy Spirit on Christ at the Jordan have?[22] Is this not a clear indication that he does not possess the divine condition? Is not the human history of Jesus, with all its changes and vicissitudes, proof that he is not God, and isn't his growth the demonstration of his personal indigence? In spite of these difficulties, Justin insists on the «newness» of what occurs in Christ, explicitly in the uniqueness of his divine Sonship announced at the Jordan, which is related to humanity's salvation, bearing in mind the intimate connection between the history of Jesus and that of humanity as a whole[23]. It is, before anything

---

21 This is such an explicit coincidence that Justin deems that the voice at Jesus' baptism, citing Ps 2:7, applied to the resurrection in Heb 13:33. Cfr. *Dial. Tryph.* 88,8 (PTS 47,224).

22 Cfr. JUSTIN, *Dial. Tryph.* 87-88 (PTS 47,220-224). Cfr. ORBE A., *La unción del Verbo*, Roma 1961, 39-82.

23 Cfr. GRANADOS J., *Los misterios de la vida de Cristo en Justino mártir* (Series: Analecta Gregoriana 296), Roma 2005, 250.

else, the newness of his manifestation to humanity: «saying that his generation [the birth of Christ] would take place for men, at the time when they would become acquainted with him»[24]. But this knowledge is not reduced to something external; rather, the goal of this birth is to allow humanity to be born for God[25]. For this to take place, Jesus himself must somehow go through the experience of birth.

The mysteries of the life of Christ show us Jesus' growth and development in his relationship with the Father. This progress in sonship, through the work of the Spirit, disposes him, on the one hand, to the realization of the mission entrusted to him. But on the other hand, Jesus must be made capable of communicating to humanity the perfection that he possesses[26]. Progression, therefore, has no other object than the perfection of humanity, but as the incarnation is presupposed, it cannot be considered meaningless for Jesus himself. And now appears the second moment in the life of Jesus that has a special significance to our purpose here: his resurrection. It appears as the moment of Jesus' «salvation»[27], «which shows that [Christ] admits them [Hebrew ancestors] to be his fathers, who trusted in God and were saved by him [cfr. Ps 22:5-6] ... and he foretells that he shall be saved by the same God, but does not boast in accomplishing anything through his own will or might»[28]. Justin also tells us the following: «For if the Son of God clearly states that he can be saved, neither because he is a son, nor because he is strong or wise, but that without God he cannot be saved [cfr. Ps 22:10-12], even though he be sinless, as Isaiah declares in words to the effect that even in regard to his very language he committed no sin "although he had done no violence, and there was no deceit in his mouth" [Is 53:9]»[29].

For Jesus, salvation means acquiring through his humanity, through his entire earthly life and especially in the resurrection, that which in a true sense, and not merely figuratively, he will give back to humanity. Christ, in his obedience to the Father until death, has imprinted in his humanity the dispositions of sonship that correspond to him and are fitting as the Son of God. As a consequence of this, in his resurrection he will also receive in his humanity, in his flesh,

---

24 JUSTIN, *Dial. Tryph.* 88,8 (PTS 47,224).

25 Cfr. GRANADOS J., *Los misterios de la vida de Cristo en Justino mártir*, 266.

26 Cfr. GRANADOS J., *Los misterios de la vida de Cristo en Justino mártir*, 269; 321-322.

27 *Dial. Tryph.* 73,2 (PTS 47,195): «was saved by resurrecting». Also 74,3 (197-198) where the passion of Christ is presented as the mystery of salvation that saved us.

28 *Dial. Tryph.* 101,1 (PTS 47,243).

29 *Dial. Tryph.* 102,7 (PTS 47,246).

the divine properties of incorruptibility and immortality. In this way, he will be able to make us participants in them as well[30]. All this will be made possible in the time and rhythm of humanity, which do not allow things to be done once for all time. Christ can be the Savior because in his humanity he has experienced and has received the salvation of God —in a word, because he has been saved. By virtue of his infinite goodness and in fulfillment of the Father's plan, the Son of God, who has not known and cannot know sin, has placed himself in the predicament of needing to be liberated and saved from death through the glory of the resurrection.

Justin is not the only one of the Fathers who has spoken of the salvation of Jesus. Hilary of Poitiers, two centuries later, and in the midst of the anti-Arian struggle, when the insistence on the humanity of Jesus gave origin to erroneous interpretations, insisted on the need for Jesus to be saved and on his solidarity with us in the weakness he shared with all of humanity: «Sharing in our common weakness he prayed the Father to save him, so that he might teach us that he was born man under all the conditions of man's infirmity»[31]. Thus Jesus invokes the name of God the Father, so that he may be saved in that humanity that he has assumed for us. Jesus first realized in himself the mystery of our salvation, and with his resurrection he annulled the decree of condemnation threatening us (cfr. Col 2:14-15): «He fulfilled the mystery of our salvation, he who coming from the dead is now eternal, first, by raising himself from the dead, and ending in himself the decree of our death, within which we were imprisoned»[32].

The salvation of Christ and our salvation are one and the same. In the glorification of Jesus' humanity, salvation is realized in him and in us. The salvation that he asks for and that takes place in him is the glorification and divinization of humanity. The spiritualization of the flesh in the resurrection is considered as the transformation of the substance of eternal salvation: «in aeternae salutem substantiam»[33]. Divinity is the *substantia salutis,* of which humanity, without ceasing to be humanity, can participate. Above all, it is the humanity of Christ, and because of it and through it, the humanity of all of us. It is the salvation that

---

30 Cfr. GRANADOS J., *Los misterios de la vida de Cristo en Justino mártir,* 338. Also pp. 443 and 468.

31 *Tr. Ps.* 53,7 (CCL 61,139); cfr. the whole context of this paragraph. Cfr. also 53,4 (131): «ut se in eo corpore, in quo erat natus… saluum faceret Dei nomen». Cfr. 68,2 (293): «The function of assumed weakness is to ask for salvation. The conscience of divinity sustains the hope for salvation after death». Cfr. BUFFER T., *Salus in Hilary of Poitiers,* Romae 2002, 179-181.

32 *Tr. Ps.* 67,23 (CCL 61,279).

33 *Tr. Ps.* 143,18 (CSEL 22,824). Cfr. also *Tr. Ps.* 139,10 (783). The Lord asks that the power of salvation be communicated to the humanity that he has assumed. *Tr. Ps.* 143,9.14 (819,822).

Jesus asks for himself as a man, the pleading of the flesh *(carnis deprecatio)*, that in the resurrection and glorification of the Lord will become for the Father what from eternity has been the Word[34]. In that glory he will be eternally contemplated by the just.

And even if it does not explicitly seem to be the vocabulary of salvation, Pope Leo the Great spoke of the exaltation of Christ in his humanity, citing the hymn of Phil 2: 6-11:

> Being uniquely the Lord Jesus Christ… nonetheless we understand that the exaltation, with which, as the peoples' Doctor says, God exalted him and gave him a name above any other (cfr. Phil 2:9-10), refers to that form which should be enriched with the increase of such a great glorification… The form of servant… through which impassive divinity carried out the mystery of great mercy (cfr. 1 Tim 3:16), is human humility, exalted in the glory of divine power[35].

On other occasions, with the insistence on the intimate relationship existing between the humanity of Jesus and the Church, the Eastern and Western fathers underlined that the sanctification and glorification that Jesus received from the Father in his humanity was destined for us all. Thus said Saint Irenaeus: «For inasmuch as the Word of God was man from the root of Jesse, and son of Abraham, in this respect did the Spirit of God rest upon him, and anoint him to preach the Gospel to the lowly (cfr. Isa 81:1; Luke 4:18)… Therefore did the Spirit of God descend upon him, [the Spirit] of him who had promised by the prophets that he would anoint him, so that we, receiving from the abundance of his unction, might be saved»[36]. Athanasius spoke in a similar fashion: «It is not the Logos as Logos and Wisdom who is anointed by the Holy Spirit he gives, rather it is the flesh assumed by him which is anointed in him and by him, so that the holiness which has come upon the Lord as man may go from him to all men»[37]. He added:

---

34 HILARY OF POITIERS, *De Trinitate* III 16 (CCL 62,88): «The Son now made flesh asked that flesh would begin to be for the Father what the Word was, so that what had begun in time would receive the glory of that aura which does not submit to time, so that the corruption of the flesh would disappear and would be transformed into God's strength and the incorruptibility of the spirit. This is the petition to God, this is the confession of the Son to the Father, and this is the beseeching of the flesh».

35 Letter *Promississe me memini* (DH 318).

36 *Adv. Haer.* III 9,3 (SCh 211,110-112). Cfr. *Demonstr.* 59 (FP 2,176).

37 ATHANASIUS OF ALEXANDRIA, *Contra Arianos* I 47 (PG 26,109). Also ibid., I 48 (113): «He sanctifies himself (cfr. John 17:10) so that we may be sanctified in him». Cfr. LADARIA L.F., «Atanasio de Alejandría y la unción de Cristo (*Contra arianos* I 47-50)» in GUIJARRO S. - FERNÁNDEZ SANGRADOR J.

«Everything Scripture says that Jesus has received is said because of his body, which is initiation of the Church … First, the Lord has raised his own body and has exalted it in itself. Then he has resurrected all its members to give them, as God, what he has received as man»[38]. The growth and development in Christ, his anointing, exaltation and glorification, do not affect his divine nature, but only his humanity, although this does not mean they do not affect him «personally» as the incarnate Son of God. But in this humanity we perceive that the whole Church, of which Christ is head, is included, which contains potentially the universality of the human race. If Jesus did not have need of salvation, once the incarnation took place for the salvation of the world, we could not imagine that the events and vicissitudes of his human life, even his death and resurrection, wouldn't have held significance for him. If this were so, the very meaning of the incarnation would be seriously compromised.

This is why tradition has spoken, albeit making due distinctions, of the salvation of Jesus—a salvation that is ours as well. The salvation Jesus experienced and received in his humanity is the one that corresponds to him as head of the body, and the one that is ultimately destined for all humanity. We can obtain this salvation through him, who, without having sinned, has been made sin for us, so that we might become the justice of God in him (cfr. 2 Cor 5:21). It does not seem exaggerated to think that the known axiom «quod non est assumptum non est sanatum»[39] gets its full meaning if we consider, in the first place, that Jesus himself has been «saved» in his humanity, which he has integrally assumed (body and soul). And because of this, the whole human race has been saved; his

---

(eds.), «*Plenitudo temporis*» *Homenaje al Prof. Dr. Ramón Trevijano Etchevarría*, Universidad Pontificia de Salamanca, Salamanca 2002, 469-479.

38 ATHANASIUS OF ALEXANDRIA, *De Incarnatione Verbi et contra Arianos* 12 (PG 26,1004). Obviously, one may notice in these and other texts from Athanasius a trend underscoring the action of Jesus as God in his humanity, with a certain forgetting of the action of the Father, who, according to the New Testament, anoints Jesus and raises him. This can be explained by the need to insist on the divinity of the Son, which was denied by Arians. But in other passages one notices greater closeness to the biblical text. Thus *De incarnatione Verbi et contra Arianos* 21 (PG 26,1021) states: «When Peter says: Let the entire house of Israel know with certainty that God has made him both Lord and Messiah this Jesus which you have crucified» (Heb 2:36), it is not of his divinity of which he says God has made Him Lord and Christ, but of his humanity which is the whole Church». A similar distinction is made by HILARY OF POITIERS in *De Trinitate* XI,19 (CCL 62A,550): «The progress produced by the anointing does not refer to what needs no growth, rather to the growth in mystery needed by progress caused by the anointing; namely, Christ is anointed so that this anointing —of the humanity he has assumed from us— would exist as sanctified (*homo noster*)».

39 «What has not been assumed has not been healed, but what is united with God is saved». Cfr. the explicit formulation of the axiom in GREGORY OF NAZIANZUS, *Ep.* 101,132 (SCh 208,50).

salvation has been passed on to all of humanity. It is clear that, in the case of Jesus, «salvation» excludes liberation from sin, which he did not commit nor could commit, but that he nevertheless bore for us. But even with the exclusion of this aspect—indeed, a point of capital importance— the sanctification, consecration, and salvation of Christ as a man are frequent themes in the theology of the fathers. Christ's entering into humanity is not even justified in many instances. The humanity of Jesus is our model and measure, because he has always fulfilled the will of the Father; it is especially in his death and resurrection, as it is in the paschal mystery that the center of the divine plan is found. Thus Jesus, perfected by obedience to the Father, is the cause of salvation for all who obey him. The humanity revivified by the Lord, who has received salvation from the Father, is the principle of the revivification of humanity[40]. There is no salvation for humanity outside of the participation in Christ's salvation.

4
God's Son in Union with Every Human Being

The fundamental premise of the soteriological lines that we have discussed, and that could be further developed, is the doctrine of the assumption of humanity as a whole by the Word, the inclusion in Christ of all humanity[41]. We are dealing with an old teaching that, rooted in the New Testament (cfr. Matt 25:31-46), has been proposed again by the Second Vatican Council: «For by His incarnation the Son of God has united himself in some fashion (*quodammodo*) with every man»[42]. «In some fashion» is a deliberately vague expression that tends to assure the impossibility of a repetition of the incarnation and the hypostatic union,

40 AMBROSE OF MILAN, *Fid.* IV 10,128-129 (*Opera* 15,314-316): «Our resemblance to the Son is stated, as well as a certain unity with him in the flesh, because as the Son of God was vivified in the flesh as man by the Father... also we as humans are vivified by the Son of God. According to this text, the generosity of grace not only reaches the human condition, but also the eternity of divinity is affirmed, it is said of divinity because it vivifies by itself, and of the human condition because it has been vivified in Christ».

41 Cfr. GONZÁLEZ DE CARDEDAL O., *Cristología* BAC, Madrid 2005, 528: «The inclusion of all humanity in Christ (creation, incarnation, redemption) is the premise of all New Testament statements about our salvation. This inclusion is the foundation of our being (as participation in his existence), of our freedom (freedom only where there is sonship), of our redemption (slavery is not overcome by self effort but by reintegration with him to the condition of sonship, to the possession of the Spirit and to the acceptance by the Father)».

42 *Gaudium et Spes* 22. Cfr. also nos. 24 and 32.

which took place once and for all times. Having reserved the unique occurrence of the incarnation of the Son, there is no reason whatsoever to interpret the expression in a minimalist sense. We cannot diminish the weight of this teaching in tradition, which has been clearly stated at times, and presupposed or implied at others. The terms used cannot give way to reductive interpretations. Bishop Irenaeus of Lyons ends his *Adversus Haereses* as follows:

> For there is the one Son, who accomplished His Father's will; and one human race also in which the mysteries of God are wrought, which the angels desire to look into (1 Pet 1:12) and they are not able to search out the wisdom of God, by means of which his handiwork, confirmed and incorporated with his Son, is brought to perfection *(per quam plasma eius conformatum et concorporatum Filio perficitur)*; that his offspring, the first-begotten Word, should descend to the creature (*facturam*), that is, to what had been molded (*plasma*), and that it should be contained by him; and, on the other hand, the creature should contain the Word, and ascend to him, passing beyond the angels *(supergrediens angelos)*, and be made after the image and likeness of God (cfr. Gen 1:26)[43].

In the descent of the Son toward us, in which he has become «co-corporeal» with each human being, there is the possibility of our ascension toward the Father, which is first realized in Christ. In this ascension, human nature goes beyond the angels, again first of all in Christ, but also in us, in the measure that we are united with him. We may acquire perfection only insofar as we conform ourselves and become «co-corporeal» with the Son of God. Human nature, in which the mysteries of God are perfected, is united with Jesus, the only Son of God, who has descended to it. With him and in him we have access to the Father, and in this consists the only definite salvation for humanity, because the vision of the Father is the life of the Son[44]. Humanity is thus united with the only Son of the Father.

43 IRENAEUS OF LYONS, *Adv. Haer.* V 36,3 (translation into Spanish by ORBE A., *Teología de San Ireneo III. Comentario al libro V del Adversus Haereses*, Madrid-Toledo 1988, 632-665). HILARY OF POITIERS, *In Matt. 6:1* (SCh 254, 170) also uses the term *concorporatio* to indicate the incarnation; in *Trin.* VI,43 (CCL 62,247) he speaks of the Son as *concarnatus*. Also the *supergrediens angelos* of Saint Irenaeus is echoed in later tradition: LEO THE GREAT, *Sermo 1 de Ascensione 4* PL 54,396: «humani generis natura... supergressura angelicos ordines, et ultra archangelorum altitudines elevanda».

44 ORBE A., *Teología de San Ireneo III. Comentario al libro V del Adversus Haereses*, 569: «Since being consubstantial with the Father as God, the Word made divine in its flesh knows the Father, those who —thanks to the salvific work of the Word— have become consubstantial with him in body and glory shall also know the Father. One and the others are, indeed, in flesh, true God. As the Logos penetrated in the flesh of paternal light, human beings, consubstantial with the Word

The parable of the lost sheep in the Gospel (cfr. Matt 18:12-14; Luke 15:4-7) provided the fathers with an opportunity to contemplate sinful humanity as a whole, which is precisely the sheep that had gone astray in Adam: saved and brought again into the flock on the shoulders of the Good Shepherd, who was sent after it upon coming into world. Once again, we may consider the words of the Bishop of Lyons:

> Wherefore also the Lord himself gave us a sign, in the depth below, and in the height above, which man did not ask for … and that what was thus born should be *God with us* (cfr. Matt 1:23; Isa 7:14), and descend to those things which are of the earth beneath, seeking the sheep which had perished, which was indeed his own peculiar handiwork, and ascend to the height above, offering and commending to his Father that human nature which had been found, making in his own person the first-fruits of the resurrection of man; that, as the head rose from the dead, so also the remaining part of the body [namely, the body] of every man who is found in life when the time is fulfilled of that condemnation which existed by reason of disobedience, may arise, blended together and strengthened through means of joints and bands (cfr. Ephesians 4:16) by the increase of God, each of the members having its own proper and fit position in the body. For there are many mansions in the Father's house (John 14:2), inasmuch as there are also many members in the body[45].

Gregory of Nyssa is even more explicit: «This sheep is humanity, who with sin has separated from the hundred reasonable sheep. The Savior takes on his shoulders the whole sheep; whole it has been restored. The Shepherd carries it

while equally glorified, shall with him, and as well, see the Father. The same light of God which until then enwrapped the flesh of the Word, shall cover —since then— his brethren, for the unity of wholeness (uncorrupted, eternal life) with Him». Cfr. ORIGEN, *In Joh.* II 2,18 (SCh 120,218).

45 IRENAEUS OF LYONS, *Adv. Haer.* III 19,3 (SCh 211,380). The very same ideas are found in HILARY OF POITIERS, *In Matt. 18:6* (SCh 258,80): «The sole sheep is to be interpreted as man and the sole man is to be interpreted as human beings, because in the loss of one, Adam, all of mankind was lost. Hence, it should be considered that the ninety nine sheep not lost are the multitude of angels who in heaven rejoice in the care and salvation of humanity. Thus, it is Christ who seeks everyone of us and the other ninety nine are the multitude in celestial glory —to which lost mankind has been returned— in the body of the Lord». Other texts from Hilary of Poitiers are rich and concise: *De Trin.* II 24 (CCL 62,60): «Made man he received from the Virgin in himself carnal nature, and through the union derived of this blend the body of the whole human race was sanctified in him. As all humans were incorporated in the body he wanted to assume, likewise, he, in turn, gave himself to all through that which is indivisible in him»; *Tr. Ps.* 51,16 (CCL 61,104): «naturam in se universae carnis adsumpsit»; 51,17 (104): «naturam… in se totius humanis generis adsumens»; 54,9 (146): «universitates nostrae caro est factus». Cfr. LADARIA L.F., *La cristología de Hilario de Poitiers,* Roma 1989, 87-103.

on his shoulders, that is, in his divinity, and by this assumption it becomes one entity with Him»[46]. Antecedents of the known statements of Saint Augustine about the «*Christus totus*», the head and members of the body, are not lacking in earlier tradition[47].

It is precisely in this line of thought that the relationship between the fulfillment of Christ and our own fulfillment is established, between the fullness he has as the head of the body and the one he himself grants to the whole body. Thus Augustine says: «When the body of the Son prays let it not separate the head from it, so that the head may be the only savior of its body, our Lord Jesus Christ Son of God, who prays for us, prays in us and is invoked by us»[48]. The rich Augustinian tradition of the Middle Ages goes even further. Christ the head is saved and only in that is he able to save his body:

«Happy are those whose transgression is forgiven, whose sin is covered» (Ps 32:1). This blest man is, no doubt Christ. Inasmuch as the head of Christ is God, it forgives sins. Inasmuch as the head of the body is only one human, nothing is forgiven to him. Inasmuch as the body of this head is formed by many, nothing is imputed against it. He, being just in himself, justifies himself. The only savior and the only saved *(solus salvator, solus salvatus)*; the only one who ascends and the only one who descends, who with the Father grants the gifts which he himself receives in men[49].

Jesus, through his divinity and consubstantiality with the Father, forgives human sins, and no one can forgive sins but God. As a human being, Jesus never personally sinned. As the inseparable head of the body of humanity that was saved by him, sin is not taken into account, thanks to the salvation he himself brought about. Given the connection with the body, he who is the savior of all of humanity is the saved one, because he does not exist without the connection to the body. Christ, who is the savior as the head of the body, is also saved as the head united inseparably to the body. There is another interesting consideration about the salvation of Christ that reappears here in a somewhat different per-

---

[46] GREGORY OF NYSSA, *Contra Apollinarem* 16 (PG 45,1153); there is also an especially significant passage from CYRIL OF ALEXANDRIA, *In Johannis Evangelium* I 9 (PG 73,161-164).
[47] Cfr. *De civ. Dei* XVII 4 (CCL 48,561-562); *En. in Ps.* 60,2; 90,2,1; 140,4 (CCL 39-40, 766; 1266; 2028).
[48] *En. in Ps.* 85,1 (CCL 39,1176).
[49] ISAAC DE LA ESTRELLA, *Sermo 42, In Ascensione Domini* 17-18 (SCh 339,52). DE LUBAC H., *Méditation sur l'Église (Oeuvres complètes* 8), Paris 2003, 156: «L'Église est en ses membres comme elle fut en son Chef: elle nést avec lui rédemptrice comme elle n'est par Lui rachetée que sur la croix».

spective than the one of the early centuries of the Church. At that time, the emphasis was on the «salvation» of Christ as a man, wholly oriented to us but personally significant to him. Now the emphasis is on the connection of the head to the body, in such a way that the fulfillment of the latter, which is caused by the head, constitutes the salvation of Christ himself, who is no longer conceivable without his body, the Church. These are two complimentary movements and not at all incompatible, one from the head to the body and the other from the body to the head.

Our salvation is that of Christ, because by virtue of the mysterious although real communion of the Son with the whole human species, what takes place in his humanity has an effect on all human beings. In him we all die and rise. But there is still a second aspect: our salvation can only take place in the fullness of his body, this fullness yet to be realized. He who is the head is also savior, insofar as he is united with the body that is also saved. In this salvation we are all called to participate. Also in this second sense, the fullness of Christ as head of the body, that is, the salvation of Christ and our salvation, with all due distinctions being made, is one and the same.

This mysterious connection between us and Christ has found one of the greatest expressions in the doctrine of exchange, which, in its precise formulation, is one of the great achievements of the theological genius of Irenaeus of Lyons: «Proper immensam suam dilectionem factus est quod sumus nos, uti nos perficeret esse quod est ipse»[50]. Due to his immense love, the Son became what we are to be: the perfection of what he is, that is, the perfection of his divine sonship. This perfection can be acquired because, as a man, he has acquired the perfection of humanity and of sonship in total execution of the will of the Father. Jesus, the Son of God, who became the Son of Man for us, is the measure of our perfection as children of God. Giving of himself for all his brothers and sisters, even unto death, Jesus gave us the yardstick of *human brotherhood* as an inseparable consequence of the divine sonship to which Jesus introduces us in the Holy Spirit.

50 IRENAEUS OF LYONS, *Adv. Haer. v Praef.* ORBE A., *Teología de San Ireneo III. Comentario al libro v del Adversus Haereses,* Madrid-Toledo 1988, 49-51. Also cfr. *Adv. Haer.* III 19,1 (SCh 211,374): «The Son of God was made man, so that man, united to the Word of God and receiving adoption, would become the Son of God… Because in what way could we join incorruption and immortality if before incorruption and immortality we would have not been made?». This passage has the value of making explicit the element of divine sonship of capital importance in Christology and in Christian anthropology. Other examples of the use of this axiom may be found in LADARIA L.F., *Teología del pecado original y de la gracia,* BAC, Madrid 2004⁴, 151.

In this mysterious exchange, Christ's salvation becomes ours, and our salvation becomes Christ's as head of the body. Nothing that takes place with the head is meaningless to the body and vice versa. This does not mean that salvation is automatic. But by virtue of the incarnation, and taking into account the differences due to each one's situation, no human being is a stranger to Christ. Therefore, in ways that only God knows, any human being can be associated by the gift of the Spirit with the paschal mystery[51]. Of course, each one can accept or refuse the gift offered in Christ. If we cannot affirm that we are all saved independently of our personal response to God, it is clear, on the other hand, that the fate of humanity as a whole is irrevocably linked to Jesus. He has given us his Spirit, who makes us the one body of his Church, but also acts outside its visible frontiers.

In the humanity of Jesus, the Spirit becomes accustomed to living among humanity: «Wherefore he also descended [the Holy Spirit] upon the Son of God, made the Son of man, becoming accustomed in fellowship with him to dwell in the human race, to rest with human beings, and to dwell in the workmanship of God, working the will of the Father in them, and renewing them from their old habits into the newness of Christ»[52]. After the glorification of Christ, the Spirit is given to all humanity as the Spirit of Christ, and he will do in us what he has done in him: carry out the will of God the Father. Due to the co-naturality, or sharing of natures, between us and Christ, the Spirit is able to communicate to us the newness of Christ. The Spirit, who has become accustomed in Christ to dwell among humanity, is now able to dwell among us, and as he has «co-naturalized»[53] Christ's humanity with God, he is also able to make our humanity co-natural with God. Also, through the entire human history of Jesus, humanity has become accustomed to receiving God, and God has become used to

---

51 Cfr. *Gaudium et Spes* 22.

52 IRENAEUS OF LYONS, *Adv. Haer.* III 17,1 (SCh 211,330). According to Irenaeus, human beings must become accustomed to bearing the Spirit and to being in communion with God. Cfr. *Adv. Haer.* IV 14,2 (SCh 100, 542-544).

53 ORBE A., *La unción del Verbo*, Roma 1961, 636-637: «In economic terms, the humanity of the Word was empowered very briefly —perhaps at the Jordan— to perform miracles and to teach. It took, however, the twelve months of public life to become capable of infusing onto others his very Spirit. Meanwhile, the Spirit slowly penetrated the soul and flesh of Jesus. More so than the assimilation of the Spirit by the humanity of Jesus, it was the assimilation of Jesus by the Spirit. In the wholeness of the Church, neither the Word as such nor *a fortiori* the simple humanity of Jesus can work with efficacy. The Word will act as principle of the Spirit —on behalf of humanity— insofar as human beings are found to be already co-naturalized, with human essences, acquired in Jesus».

dwelling among humanity[54]. What takes place in the humanity of Jesus also has a meaning for us by virtue of his union with all of humanity and the outpouring of the Spirit. The Holy Spirit is the link between the «salvation» of Jesus and our own.

5

Eschatological Perspectives

⌘

In our brief survey on the relationship between the «salvation» of Christ and our own, we must give some consideration to the final consummation and to the *parousia* of the Lord. We have already referred to some New Testament passages dealing with the final victory of Christ over all enemies. This victory has been assured by the resurrection and is related to the fullness of Christ, and consequently to our own. But it has not yet reached consummation. A very well-known passage written by Origen links the fullness of Christ with that of his body, which is the whole Church:

> Now my savior is afflicted by my sins. My savior cannot rejoice: I shall drink, he says, this wine with you in the kingdom of my father because I remain in iniquity. How could he rejoice, he who approaches the altar of propitiation for me, sinner, he whose heart is continuously saddened by my errors? I shall drink, he says, this wine with you in the kingdom of my Father (cfr. Matt 26:29). Since we do not yet behave so that we would rise to the Kingdom, he who has promised to drink this wine with us cannot drink this wine. He who has taken our wounds upon himself and has suffered for our cause as physician of our souls and bodies, would he forget now the corruption of our sores? … Thus, he waits for us to convert, to imitate his example, to follow his footsteps, in order to rejoice with us and to drink with us the wine in the Kingdom of his Father … He does not want to drink alone the wine of the Kingdom. He awaits us, because he

---

54 IRENAEUS OF LYONS, *Adv. Haer.* III 20,2 (SCh 211,392): «He, the Word of God who inhabited mankind and became son of man to train humans in welcoming God and train God in inhabiting humans, in keeping with the pleasure of the Father»; cfr. also *Adv. Haer.* III 18,7 (364-366): «The mediator between God and mankind, thanks to the familiarity among them, had to redirect them to friendship and concord and to achieve the assumption of humanity by God and the self-offering of humanity to God. Indeed, how would we have received communion of him and with him, had his Word not entered in communion with us by becoming flesh?». Cfr. ORBE A., *Introducción a la teología de los siglos II y III*, Roma 1987, 670-671.

has said: until I drink it with you (cfr. Matt 26:29). Abandoning ourselves in our lives we delay his joy … He shall drink it again later when all things shall be submitted to him, and, all being saved and the death of sin destroyed, it will not be necessary to offer victims for sin… You shall have joy when you leave this life if you have been holy. But your joy shall only be complete when no member of your body is missing. Because you will await others like you, you, yourself, have waited[55].

It is clear that we cannot forget —as, indeed, it has not been forgotten by tradition— that Jesus lives resurrected, in the fullness of divine glory, seated at the right hand of the Father. It is obvious that utmost caution is necessary in the interpretation of these texts. But we cannot despise these intuitions. Jesus, who is already seated at the right of the Father, waits for his enemies to be brought to his feet in order to deliver the Kingdom to him (cfr. 1 Cor 15:25-28). Jesus intercedes for us before the Father, and in him we have a high priest who, tested in suffering, may be compassionate toward our weaknesses (cfr. Heb 2:17-18; 4:14-16). By virtue of this compassion, in a way that is indeed mysterious to us, Jesus takes upon himself our pain and frailty. Until the moment of final consummation, neither the pain of humanity, whose wounds he came to heal, nor the sins of humanity, for which he intercedes before the Father, can be without meaning for Jesus.

Saint Augustine reminded us of the identification of Jesus with those who suffer persecution or have any type of need: «He has already been exalted above the heavens, but he suffers on earth the pain we experience as his members. Of this he gives testimony claiming from above: "Saul, Saul, why do you persecute me?" (Acts 9:4), and "I was hungry, and you gave me food" (Matt 25:35)»[56]. The last lines in the Origen text apply to humanity what had been said of Jesus. Joy will be complete when no member of the body of Christ is lacking, which will then become the body of all. The fullness of Christ will coincide with that of our fullness. Saint Thomas spoke of the communion of all the blessed as an impor-

---

55 ORIGEN, *Hom. in Leviticum* 7,2 (SCₕ 286,308-316).
56 AUGUSTINE, *Sermo mai. 98. De Ascensione Domini* 1 (PLS 494). In the Middle Ages, these ideas were repeated while citing the same biblical texts as Saint Augustine. Thus, ISAAC DE LA ESTRELLA, *Sermo* 42,11 (SCₕ 239,44), when speaking of the identification of Jesus with those who suffer, asks: «For what reason, other than the union between the husband and the wife, or the head and the body?». In today's theology we find interesting echoes of this ancient tradition. GONZÁLEZ DE CARDEDAL O., *Cristología*, BAC, Madrid 2005, 488. «[Christ] remains in agonic struggle until all of us participate in his victory. Glorified, he no longer dies, but he is not fully glorified as long as one member of his body, yet a pilgrim, is still subjected to the insecurity of history. The Messiah is yet to come definitively».

tant element in eternal life. «This communion shall be very pleasing, because each one will love the other as himself and will rejoice in the good of the other as in his own»[57]. The fullness of the body of Christ is, in the previously mentioned sense, the fullness of Christ himself, and at the same time this fullness is that of each human being. The fulfillment of God's design in Christ and our salvation are intimately linked. The Kingdom of Christ will include all saved human beings. The final fulfillment of this kingdom delivered by Christ to the Father at the end of times will also mean that human beings will reign together with the Lord: «He himself shall deliver [to the Father] as kingdom those who will reign with him»[58]. «When this David [Christ] is liberated and he is no longer subjected to the law of death, salvation is also granted to kings … His liberation is the salvation of kings. These will reign conformed to his glory»[59]. The Kingdom of Christ and ours coincide. His «salvation» and ours are the same thing.

This Christological dimension has not always been taken into account in the very lively discussion that took place some years ago on the «intermediate state» that centered on all anthropological issues. But this aspect of the fullness of the body of Christ, which is present in tradition, cannot be forgotten. It shows anew that the theme of salvation cannot be dealt with theologically, without keeping in mind the unique and universal mediation of Jesus. A salvation that is marginal to the fullness of the heavenly Church, the risen body of Christ, is not contemplated either in the New Testament or in the tradition of the Church.

In the eschatological studies of the past few decades, the question of the eternal meaning of the humanity of Christ in our relationship with God is likewise intimately linked to this issue. Does this humanity have an eternal function and significance? Given the incarnation, the exclusive fruit of divine love and generosity, the exaltation of Christ in his humanity becomes «necessary», because this humanity remains united with the Word existing in the person of Christ[60], and therefore, definitely enters the divine life. «Quod semel adsumpsit nunquam dimisit» is one of the implicit premises of Christology and Christian soteriology[61]. If the glorified humanity of Christ were to vanish, if this «saved» human-

---

57 *Opusc. Theol.* 2
58 HILARY OF POITIERS, *Tr. Ps.* 139,17 (CSEL 22,788).
59 HILARY OF POITIERS, *Tr. Ps.* 133,21 (CSEL 22,826); 149,4 (969): «Nos secum adsumpsit in reges».
60 Cfr. THOMAS AQUINAS, *STh.* III 2,2; III 2,3. Inasmuch as it subsists in two natures, the person of Christ is «composita»; III 17,2, the divine person does not subsist only in keeping with divine nature, but also in keeping with human nature.
61 Cfr. ORBE A., *En torno a la encarnación*, Aldecoa, Burgos 1985, 205-219.

ity would not exist forever, then the *raison d'être* of our hope would disappear as well. Our humanity will endure forever due to its insertion into the body of the risen Christ. In 1953, Karl Rahner wrote a brief article, which later became famous, on this argument[62]. The German theologian reached the conclusion that, in eternal life, the Father can be contemplated only through the Son, but in this way he is immediately contemplated, because the immediacy of the vision of God does not deny the eternal mediation of Christ as a human being. It should be kept in mind that the fourth gospel speaks of a revealing function of the glorified Christ, in the profound relationship existing between the revelation of the Father by Jesus and the glorification of Christ by the Father (cfr. John 17:24-26): «Christ is constitutively revealer of the Father, but he does not reveal him fully and perfectly until the resurrection when his humanity reaches the glorious state, in which he will glow, and his character as eternal Word of the Father shall be fully manifested; then, in the vision of his glory men glorified with him shall have the vision of the Father: fully revealing himself, Christ will fully reveal the Father»[63]. While Jesus does not have the perfect glory of the Father, he cannot fully reveal him, and until human beings are glorified themselves, they will not be ready to fully grasp this revelation in all of its depth.

The revelation of the Father does not only occur through the glorious humanity of Jesus, but also in it, insofar as we are inserted into his risen body. Our resurrection will take place in the body of Christ, through whom we have access to the Father. To be conquered by Christ (cfr. Phil 3:12) means «to be found in that body he assumed from us, in which we have been chosen before the creation of the world (cfr. Eph 1:4), in which we have been reconciled, whereas before we were enemies»[64]. The humanity of Christ not only endures in eternal life; it is also the place of our encounter with God.

62 RAHNER K., «Eterna significación de la humanidad de Jesús para nuestra relación con Dios» in *Escritos de teología III*, Madrid 1967, 47-59; this article appeared for the first time in German, entitled «Die ewige Bedeutung der Menschheit Jesu für unser Gottverhältnis» in *Geist und Leben* 26 (1953) 279-288, and later in *Volume III* of his *Scriften zur Theologie* (1960).

63 ALFARO J., «Cristo glorioso, revelador del Padre» in RAHNER K., *Cristología y Antropología*, Madrid 1973, 141-182, 169. In recent years, these intuitions have been widely assumed in Catholic eschatology.

64 HILARY OF POITIERS, *Tr. Ps.* 13,3 (CCL 61,79); 15,4 (84): «…si tamen nos uitia corporis nostri cruci eius confixerimus ut in eius corpore resurgamus». Cfr. LADARIA L.F., *La Cristología de Hilario de Poitiers*, Roma 1989, 99; 283-286. Cfr. also ORBE A., «Visión del Padre e incorruptela según San Ireneo» in *Gregorianum* 64 (1983) 199-241, especially 207-209.

Mediation, in Christ's case, does not mean the presence of an intermediary who becomes superfluous once those he wished to unite have come to an agreement. The mediation of Jesus is not that of one who is between God and us. On the contrary, in him and for him, our immediacy with the Father takes place. There is no other way to attain it; no one goes to the Father other than through him (cfr. John 14:6), and this path does not become superfluous because the goal has been achieved. In Christ we enter into communion with God. In the power of his Spirit we are already —and we will be even more fully— children of God. Salvation cannot consist in moving away from Christ to get to God, but in participating ever more intensely in his life. We will never «overcome» our condition of the image of the heavenly man —neither our conformation with him nor our divine sonship.

When Irenaeus repeats to us that the goal and ultimate finality of human life is the vision of God *paternaliter*[65], he is saying that the personal relationship with the one who is by nature the first begotten will always be meaningful for us. Divine fatherhood will always refer primarily to the Son. The Son's risen body is the setting of our eternal life, the participation in the salvation that he, as God and man, has obtained in his humanity for all of us. Without any gain for his divine person, who lives forever in the fullness of the exchange of love with the Father and the Holy Spirit, he has assumed human nature as his own and does not live without it in communion with the other persons of the Trinity. In this exchange humanity has been incorporated by virtue of the incarnation, death, and resurrection of the Son of God. The fullness of this gift of the Spirit of the risen one will perfect us in our divine sonship: «For if the promise of things to come, gathering humanity into himself, even now causes him to cry, *Abba, Father* (Rom 8:15; Gal 4:6), what shall the complete grace of the Spirit effect, which shall be given to men by God? It will render us like him, and accomplish the will of the Father; for it shall make man after the image and likeness of God (cfr. Gen 1:16)»[66]. The vision of God supposes that this fatherhood extends to all human

---

65 Cfr. IRENAEUS OF LYONS, *Adv. Haer.* IV 20,5 (SCh 100,638): V 36,3 (ORBE A., *Teología de San Ireneo III. Comentario al libro v del Adversus Haereses,* Madrid-Toledo 1988, 622-629): «In all of this and through it all God the Father reveals himself, who shapes man and promised the fathers the inheritance of earth; manifested in the resurrection of the just and promises fulfilled in the Kingdom of his Son. Later, He grants, as Father, that "what no eye has seen, nor ear heard, nor the human heart conceived" (1 Cor 2:9)».

66 IRENAEUS OF LYONS, *Adv. Haer.* V 8,1 (cfr. ORBE A., *Teología de San Ireneo III. Comentario al libro v del Adversus Haereses,* Madrid-Toledo 1988, 374-377).

beings saved by Christ. The Second Vatican Council says in *Ad Gentes* 7: «And so at last, there will be realized the plan of our Creator who formed man in His own image and likeness, when all who share one human nature, regenerated in Christ through the Holy Spirit and beholding the glory of God, will be able to say with one accord: "Our Father"».

Christ is, therefore, our salvation, not only because he liberates us from evil, but because in him, the perfect human being, our salvation is measured with the yardstick of God himself and the divine life that Jesus possesses for all eternity.

6

Offering Salvation

The offer of salvation, of which Christianity is the vehicle, is thus founded in Christ in a very profound way. This is not only because Christ alone is the savior, who by his death and resurrection has liberated humanity from sin and has communicated his divine life to us, but also because the «salvation» he has communicated is his very own —the salvation that he, in his humanity, received from the Father, who, as we have seen, is also the savior of humanity according to the New Testament. He wishes to share this salvation with all of us; what is more, he does not want to have it without us, because he does not want, as the head, to be without the body.

This offer of salvation is for all human beings, without exception; the announcement of Christ is extended to everybody. It is an announcement of which the vehicle is the Church, the pilgrim Church whose very nature is missionary, as the Second Vatican Council teaches (cfr. *Ad Gentes* 2;6). John Paul II pointed out this idea in *Redemptoris Missio* 5: «In this definitive Word of his revelation, God has made himself known in the fullest possible way. He has revealed to humankind *who he is*. This definitive self-revelation of God is the fundamental reason why the Church is missionary by her very nature». Christ's salvation and its announcement are intimately linked to the full revelation that God makes of himself in Christ.

But the good news of Christ and his saving work has not, in fact, reached all human beings, to whom it is destined. This does not mean that the salvation of Jesus will not reach them. It will suffice to remember a central affirmation of Vatican II, as stated in *Gaudium et Spes* 22: «For, since Christ died for all men, and since the ultimate vocation of man is in fact one, and divine, we ought to believe that the Holy Spirit in a manner known only to God offers to every man the possibility of being associated with this paschal mystery»[67]. In these times of pluralism, it may be striking that the Church insists on maintaining the unique and universal character of the salvation of Christ. This is not the time to repeat the statements from the Bible and the Church's tradition referred to at the onset of our presentation, in which the recent affirmations of the Church's teaching are founded[68]—statements, by the way, that demonstrate appreciation and recognition of the values found in those who do not share our faith, in different cultures, and in other religions of the world[69]. In them, too, are found the seed of the Word and the rays of the truth that is Christ. This acknowledgement is a very important aspect of the proclamation of the unity and universality of Christ's salvation. It reminds us that this universality includes more than it excludes, among other reasons because the unique mediation of Jesus cannot be separated from God's will of universal salvation (cfr. 1 Tim 2:3-5).

The previous reflections will have shown one of the reasons for the coherence of this viewpoint. Christ, united with all of humanity, wishes to make all of us participants in the life and fullness that he didn't want to have without us, this life that he received from the Father. If we are all called to this end, we cannot think that there may be diverse paths to reach it. It is not a matter of Jesus giving us just any salvation. The person of the Savior, the Son of God made man, who died and rose for us, essentially determines salvation itself. This is what the anonymous author of the so-called second letter of Clement anticipated appropriately: «We have to think of Jesus Christ as God so as not to hold in low esteem our salvation»[70]. We Christians cannot have low esteem either for our salvation or for that of others. To this we are guided by the love for all humanity that Christ taught us.

---

67 Cfr. ORBE A., *Teología de San Ireneo III. Comentario al libro v del Adversus Haereses,* Madrid-Toledo 1988, 24;29. God has called all human beings to the same destiny; there is no other end for humanity but God himself. Humanity is called to attain this destiny.

68 Cfr. *Redemptoris Missio* 5-6.10; *Dominus Iesus* 13-15, among other places.

69 Cfr. *Redemptoris Missio* 5-6; 28-29; 55-56; *Dominus Iesus* 8; 12.

70 CLEMENT OF ALEXANDRIA, 2 *Clem.* 11 (FP 4,174). AMBROSE OF MILAN, *De Fide IV* 10,130 (*Opera* 15,316), said the same thing with words that were not devoid of irony: «Arians can have the reward of their faith, or it may be that they receive the eternal life of the Son». Cfr. NOVO CID-FUENTES A., *Los misterios de la vida de Cristo en Ambrosio de Milán,* Instituto Teológico Compostelano, Santiago de Compostela 2003, 298.

God's Incarnation and Christian Theology of Religion

«Long ago God spoke to our ancestors in many and various ways by the prophets, but in these last days he has spoken to us by a Son, whom he appointed heir of all things, through whom he also created the worlds» (Heb 1:1-2). If the constant presence of God in the world and his closeness to humanity has been a Christian conviction from early times (Acts 17:27: «indeed he is not far from each one of us»), then it is equally clear that in Christ this closeness has reached its maximum and unsurpassable degree[1]. When God spoke to us through the Son, through his whole life, death, and resurrection, he used a language qualitatively superior to any other. Indeed, in no other way has it been revealed, in all its depth, exactly who God is than through the love he showed for us by sending his Son into the world. In the incarnation of the Son, as well as his whole life, the mystery of God's love for humanity is revealed in a totally unsuspected way. «He delivered the Son to free the enslaved», sings the paschal liturgy. «But God proves his love for us in that this: while we still were sinners, Christ died for us» (Rom 5:8). «God so loved the world that He sent His only Son» (John 3:16). The revelation of the love of God the Father is possible, because in Christ, the image of the invisible God, in whom we see the Father himself, he has loved us to the extreme. The love of Christ is a demonstration of the love of the Father. Christ is truly God with us in the participation of our whole life, tested in everything, like us in all things except sin (cfr. Heb 4:15). With his presence, sent «as man to all human beings»[2], the Son has revealed God to us and has brought us his salvation.

But the presence of Christ in the world did not end with his mortal life. Moreover, it has become, after his resurrection and ascension into heaven, more universal, although obviously more mysterious. «I am with you always, to the end of the age» (Matt 28:20). Christ refers, above all, to disciples who always rejoice in his presence and protection, especially in difficult times. But the risen Lord encompasses everything and the action of his Spirit knows no limits. The Church, the Body of Christ, is the place *par excellence* where this presence of Christ and his Spirit reside, but it is not the only place. When the issue of the theology of religions is dealt with, the central premise of the universal action of Christ and his Spirit cannot be forgotten. The time for a narrow understanding of the need of belonging to the Church for salvation has come and gone. The possibility of

---

1 Cfr. the essay of LADARIA L.F. about this theme published in CORDOVILLA PÉREZ A. - SÁNCHEZ CARO J.M. - DEL CURA ELENA S. (eds.), *Dios y el hombre en Cristo. Homenaje a Olegario González de Cardedal. Sígueme,* Salamanca, 2006, 223-243.
2 *To Diogneto* 7,4 (SCh 33ff., 68).

salvation outside the visible frontiers of the Church is a fact, not only in Catholic theology but in the Church's teachings as well. But neither the Church, to which everything is ordered, nor the far greater reason of Christ being the sole mediator, are absent from this salvation. If the possibility of salvation for all human beings is not an issue in theological discussion today, in spite of the qualified magisterial interventions, the debate on the universality of Christ's mediation in salvation is not closed[3].

It is not necessary to look into all of the different schools and theories of the past years to consider this issue. I would like to reflect only on the relevance of the incarnation, the ultimate expression of God's love for humanity, for the salvation of all. The unique event of the coming of God into the world cannot but have a universal significance. The Church has always understood it in this way.

1

The Incarnation: A Unique and Non-Repeatable Event

God's universal will for salvation and the unique mediation of Christ, who gave himself for our deliverance, are explicitly linked in the New Testament (cfr. 1 Tim 2:3-6). Jesus came to expunge sin from the world (cfr. John 1:29); in him God has reconciled the world to himself (cfr. 2 Cor 5:18-19). The coming of the Son of God into this world is in itself a saving event, with positive effects for all. With the incarnation of the Word comes all its newness, in spite of the prophetic announcement that anticipated everything, according to Irenaeus[4]. This is a unique

---

3   The bibliography on this question is voluminous. Without pretending to be exhaustive, we point to MENKE K.H., *Die Einzigkeit Jesu Christ im Horizont der Sinnfrage,* Einsiedeln-Freiburg 1995; GEFFRÉ C., «Pour un Christianisme mondial» in *Recherches de Science Religieuse* 86 (1998) 53-75; DE FRANCA MIRANDA M., *O cristianismo em face das religioes,* Sao Paulo 1998; SCHULZ M., «Anfragen an die pluralistische Religions-theologie: Einer ist Gott, nur Einer auch Mittler», *Münchener theologische Zeitschrift* 51 (2000) 125-150; IAMMARRONE G., «La dottrina del primato assoluto e della signoria universale di Gesù Cristo nel dibattito attuale sul valore salvifico delle religioni» in SANNA I. (ed)., *Gesù Cristo speranza del mondo,* Roma 2000, 339-408; MÜLLER G.L. - SERRETTI M. (eds.), *Einzigkeit und Universalität Jesu Christi im Dialog mit den Religionen,* Einsiedeln 2000; DHAVAMONY M., «The Uniqueness and Universality of Jesus Christ» in *Studia Missionalia* 50 (2001) 179-216; AMATO A., «La universalidad salvífica del misterio de la encarnación» en PRADES J. (ed.), *El misterio a través de las formas,* Facultad de Teología San Dámaso, Madrid 2002, 143-161; DUQUOC C., *L'unico Cristo. La sinfonia differita,* Brescia 2003; GÄDE G., *Cristo nelle religioni,* Roma 2004; MAZUR A., *L'insegnamento di Giovanni Paolo II sulle altre religioni,* Roma 2004; DHAVAMONY M., *World Religions in the History of Salvation,* Washington 2004.
4   Cfr. IRENAEUS OF LYONS, *Adv. Haer.* IV 34,1 (SCh 100,846-848).

and unrepeatable occurrence. The New Testament maintains, as it is well known, that the redemptive action of Christ happened only once, and for all times (cfr. Heb 7:27; 9:12, 26-28; 10:10; 1 Pet 3:18). The uniqueness of Christ's sacrifice should be seen in intimate relationship with the uniqueness of the incarnation. The Son came into the world only once to liberate us from sin. His glorious coming at the end of times will not be a repetition of this event. It will be the total expression of his complete dominion and the victory over sin that he already achieved through his death and resurrection. The Son was incarnated only once, and only once did he offer himself as a ransom for all by shedding his blood on the cross. There is no other mediator and no other sacrifice. The uniqueness of Christ's mediation in salvation, a conviction repeatedly expressed in the New Testament (cfr. Acts 4:12; John 3:16-17; 14:6), impelled the authors of the New Testament to speak of the mediation of the only Lord, Jesus Christ, at creation (cfr. 1 Cor 8:6; Col 1:15-17; John 1:3, 10; Heb 1:2). Thus, a deep link is clearly established, although implicitly, between the salvation that Christ brought to the world and the totality of creation, and in a particular way humanity. Christ must be preached to all humanity, because all of us are the beneficiaries of his salvation, and therefore beneficiaries of his message.

Hence, Christ has a universal relevance. Christians have read history based on this event. One of the initial problems to be faced was that of the unity of the history of salvation, and therefore of the «identity» of the God who repeatedly manifested himself in the Old Testament. God the Creator and God the Father of Jesus are one and the same; he made himself present to humanity from the beginning of time through his Son. If the Son of God has become our brother, if he has shared our condition, then the closeness of God to his people during the entire history of Israel has been an anticipation of the incarnation, which gives history its definitive meaning: «… and all drank the same spiritual drink. For they drank from the spiritual rock that followed them, and the rock was Christ» (1 Cor 10:4). The fathers of the first centuries attributed to the Son the theophanies found in the Old Testament[5]. If it is the Son who was incarnated, then God

---

5 Cfr. JUSTIN, *Apol.* I 62-63 (Wartelle, 184-186); *Dial. Triph.* 56-62. (Marcovich 161-164); THEOPHILUS OF ANTIOCH, *Ad. Autol.* II 22 (SCh 20,154); IRENAEUS OF LYONS, *Adv. Haer.* IV 5,2; 7,4; 20,7-11 (SCh 100,428-430;462;646-662); CLEMENT OF ALEXANDRIA, *Ped.* I 7,57,2 (SCh 70,212); *Strom.* V 6,34,1 (SCh 278,80); VII 10,58,3 (SCh 428,188-190); *Exc. Ex Theod.* 10,5; 12,1; 23,5, the Son was only visible to angels (SCh 23,78-80;82;108); TERTULLIAN, *Adv. Prax.* XIV-XVI (Scarpat 178-190); *Adv. Marc.* II 27,3-5; III 6-7 (CCL 1, 506; 514-518); NOVATIAN, *Trin.* XVIII-XIX (CCL 4,44-50); HILARY OF POITIERS, *Trin.* IV 27-42; V 11-22 (CCL 62,130-149; 160-173), among many others. Still, Leo the Great, after Saint Augustine changed the traditional position, maintained older viewpoints: *Ep.* 31,2 (PL 54,971).

has always made himself visible through him. «*Visibile Patris Filius*»—that which is visible of the Father is the Son, according to Irenaeus[6]. This bishop of Lyons insisted that by the will of the Father the Word of God has always been with human beings and has accompanied them: «*semper humani generi adest*»[7].

Saints Justin and Clement of Alexandria have spoken of the Logos, of whom the whole human species can in some way participate, but which is fully expressed only in Christ, so that only Christians may know him entirely[8]. Thus, we cannot think of a divine action, such as salvation or creation, as wholly unrelated to the incarnation and the entire life of Jesus of Nazareth, especially his paschal mystery. Jesus is the beginning and the end (Rev 22:13); he is «the goal of human history, the focal point of the longings of history and of civilization, the center of the human race, the joy of every heart and the answer to all its yearnings»[9]. Jesus is the one who gives history its definitive meaning, because, having entered it, he gives it a transcendent dimension. The incarnation of the Son has revealed to us who God is when he himself entered human history, and from the death and resurrection of Jesus this history has received both its meaning and definitive direction: to move toward the recapitulation in Christ of all things, those in heaven and those on earth (cfr. Eph 1:10).

---

6 IRENAEUS OF LYONS, *Adv. Haer.* IV 6,6 (SCh 100,450).

7 IRENAEUS OF LYONS, *Adv. Haer.* III 16,6 (SCh 211,312); Cfr. also III 18,1 (342); IV 6,7; 20,4; 28,2 (SCh 100,454; 634-636; 758); V 16,1 (SCh 153,214); *Demonstr.* 12 (FP 2, 81-82).

8 JUSTIN, *Apology* I 46, 2 (Wartelle, 160): «We have received the teaching that Christ is the firstborn of God, and before we have indicated that he is the Word, of whom the whole human species has been a part»; II 8,3 (208): «It is not any marvel, if [demons] become unmasked, they attempt to make ever more hideous those who live not only in conformity with the seminal Word, but likewise in conformity with the knowledge and contemplation of the total Word, who is Christ». Ladaria uses the Spanish translations by RUIZ BUENO D., BAC, 232; 209. Cfr. CLEMENT OF ALEXANDRIA, *Protr.* I 6,4; X 98,4 (SCh 2 bis 60; 166); *Paed.* I 11,96 (SCh 70,280).

9 *Gaudium et Spes* 45. Cfr. PAUL VI, *aloc.* February 3, 1965. Also: *Gaudium et Spes* 10: «The Church believes that Christ, dead and risen for all, gives humans his light and strength by the Holy Spirit, so that they may respond to their ultimate vocation, and that no other name, under heaven, has been given to humanity necessary to be saved (cfr. Acts 4:12). Likewise, the Church believes that the key, the core, and the end of all human history are to be found in the Lord and Master». JOHN PAUL II, *Redemptoris Missio* 6: «This unique singularity of Christ renders him an absolute and universal meaning, by virtue of which, while being in history, he is the center and the end of said history: "I am the Alpha and the Omega, the first and last, the beginning and the end" (Rev 22:13)».

2

«The Son of God Is Somehow in Union with Every Human Being»

The fact that the Son of God became a human being and entered human history has great significance for each and every one of us. The Logos is the light that enlightens every human who comes into the world (cfr. John 1:9)[10]. The light that is the incarnate Word comes to all, even though we do not always know how. On the other hand, the Incarnation did not diminish the divinity of the Son, nor has it eliminated or diminished his humanity; rather, it has exalted it: «*humana augens, divina non minuens*», said Saint Leo the Great in one of his well-known formulations[11]. And what in the beginning was thought to be an expression of the dignity of the human nature of the Lord may now be extended, without in any way forcing the term, to the human species in its totality. The Second Vatican Council states: «Since human nature as he assumed it was not annulled, by that very fact it has been raised up to a divine dignity in our respect too. For by his incarnation the Son of God has united himself in some fashion *(quodammodo)* with every human being» (*Gaudium et Spes* 22)[12]. The elevation of human nature takes place not only in Christ, who has assumed it in his very person (union, according to *hypostasis*), but also in every one of us. The reason for this is the mysterious union (mysterious does not mean less real) of Christ with every human being through the incarnation[13].

Vatican II recounts in more personal terms what has been a very frequent doctrine of the fathers of the Church, who have repeatedly taught that Christ, by incarnating, has become united with the whole of human nature. This union constitutes the premise of our participation in the life of the glorious Christ, raised with him and in him to divine life.

---

10 The translation of this text in the Vulgate says: «… qui illuminat omnem hominem venientem in mundum». But this is not the interpretation favored by many authorized exegetes. The illumination of all humans should be related with the coming of the Logos into this world. The New Vulgate has translated the text with the words «…veniens in mundum».

11 *Tomus ad Flavianum* (DH 293).

12 The text continues as follows: «He worked with human hands, he thought with human intelligence, he loved with a human heart. Born of the Virgin Mary he truly became one of us, similar to us in everything except in sin» Cfr. also *Gaudium et Spes* 24;32. Also: JOHN PAUL II, *Redemptoris hominis* 13.

13 «The more deeply Jesus Christ descends in the participation of human misery, the higher human beings ascend in the participation of divine life». COMISIÓN TEOLÓGICA INTERNACIONAL, *Documentos 1969-1996*, POZO C., S.J. (ed.) BAC, Madrid 1998, I E 4, Madrid 1998, 254.

Irenaeus, one of the great representatives of this tradition, closes with these words in his treatise against heresies:

For there is the one Son, who accomplished his Father's will; and one human race also in which the mysteries of God are wrought, «things into which angels long to look» (1 Pet 1:12); and they are not able to search out the wisdom of God, by means of which his handiwork, confirmed and incorporated with his Son *(conformatum et concorporatum Filio)*, is brought to perfection; that his offspring, the first-begotten Word, should descend to the creature *(facturam)*, that is, to what had been molded (*plasma*), and that it should be contained by him; and, on the other hand, the creature should contain the Word, and ascend to him, passing beyond the angels *(supergrediens angelos)*[14], and be made after the image and likeness of God [likewise, he reveals himself] one only Son, who fulfilled the will of the Father (cfr. Gen 1:26)[15].

Cyril of Alexandria comments on John 1:14 as follows:

For we were all in Christ, and the community of human nature mounteth up unto his person … The Word then dwelt in all through one that the One being declared the Son of God with power according to the Spirit of holiness (cfr. Rom 1:4), the dignity might come unto all human nature and thus because of One of us, «I say, You are gods, children of the Most High, all of you» (cfr. Ps 82:6; John 10:34), it might come to us also. Is it not clear to all, that he descended unto the condition of bondage, not himself giving thereby anything to himself, but bestowing himself on us, that we through his poverty might be rich (cfr. 2 Cor 8:9), and soaring up through likeness to him unto his own special good, might be made gods and children of God through faith? For he who is by nature Son and God dwelt in us, wherefore in his Spirit do we cry «Abba

---

14 LEO THE GREAT seems to echo this formula in his *Sermo 1 de Ascensione* 4 (PL 54,396): «humani generis natura… supergressura angelicos ordines».

15 IRENAEUS OF LYONS, *Adv. Haer.* V 36,3. Translation by ORBE A., *Teología de San Ireneo. Comentario al libro V del «Adversus Haereses»* III, Madrid-Toledo 1988, 633-655. One can also see the extensive commentary on the text on the union of Christ with all humans in *Adv. Haer.* V 15,2, in terms of the Parable of the Lost Sheep. Cfr. ORBE A., *Teología de San Ireneo. Comentario al libro V del «Adversus Haereses»* II, Madrid-Toledo 1987, 46-47. This parable has been frequently interpreted in the sense that all of humanity is the lost sheep that Jesus carries on his shoulders when he incarnated in order to take it to paradise; cfr. for example HILARY OF POITIERS, *In Mat.* 18,6 (SCh 254,80); *Tract. Myst.* I 18 (SCh 19 bis, 106-108); GREGORY OF NYSSA, *Contra Apoll.* 16 (PG 45,1153): «This sheep is we, humans, who have become estranged by sin from the hundred reasonable sheep. The Savior carries on his shoulders the whole flock, as it was not totally lost. As it had been lost completely, so it has been completely taken to paradise. The Shepherd carries it on his shoulders, namely, in his divinity».

Father» (Rom 8:15; Gal 4:6). And the Word dwells in one temple taken for our sakes and of us, as in all, in order that having all in himself, he might reconcile all in one body unto the Father, as Paul says (cfr. Eph 2:16)[16].

As we have previously cited in the text of Saint Irenaeus[17], it explains, perhaps with greater clarity, how the union with all of humanity constitutes the basis and foundation that Christ, by virtue of his death and resurrection, could give us the gift of the Spirit, could make us his children in him, could make us divine. The fact that the Son of God became a human being and shared our condition affects all of us. The old theology of exchange, which is so close to what we have just considered, underscores it: «Our Lord Jesus Christ… through his transcendent love (cfr. Eph 3:19), becomes what we are, that he might bring us to be even what he is himself, our Lord Jesus Christ»[18].

The salvation of humanity cannot be other than a participation in the life of Christ. It has its sole basis, within the only existing saving order, in the communication of the divine life of Jesus, who, having died and risen, gives us his glorified humanity, which he first received from Mary through the action of the Holy Spirit.

---

16 CYRIL OF ALEXANDRIA, *In Joh. Evang.* I 9 (PG 73,161-164). One may remember some of the formulations of HILARY OF POITIERS, *In Mt.* 19,5 (SCh 258,94): «omnium nostrum corpus adsumpsit»; *Tr. Ps.* 54,9 (CCL 61,146): «universitatis nostrae caro est factus».

17 Cfr. Chapter 3 of the present Volume. IRENAEUS OF LYONS, *Adv. Haer.* V 36,3. Translation by ORBE A., *Teología de San Ireneo. Comentario al libro V del «Adversus Haereses»* III, Madrid-Toledo 1988, 633-655. One can also see the extensive commentary on the text on the union of Christ with all humans in *Adv. Haer.* V 15,2, in terms of the Parable of the Lost Sheep. Cfr. ORBE A., *Teología de San Ireneo. Comentario al libro V del «Adversus Haereses»* II, Madrid-Toledo 1987, 46-47. This parable has been frequently interpreted in the sense that all of humanity is the lost sheep that Jesus carries on his shoulders when he incarnated in order to take it to paradise; cfr. for example HILARY OF POITIERS, *In Mat.* 18,6 (SCh 254,80); *Tract. Myst.* I 18 (SCh 19 bis, 106-108); GREGORY OF NYSSA, *Contra Apoll.* 16 (PG 45,1153): «This sheep is we, humans, who have become estranged by sin from the hundred reasonable sheep. The Savior carries on his shoulders the whole flock, as it was not totally lost. As it had been lost completely, so it has been completely taken to paradise. The Shepherd carries it on his shoulders, namely, in his divinity».

18 IRENAEUS OF LYONS, *Adv. Haer.* V praef.; cfr. ORBE A., *Teología de San Ireneo* I, Madrid-Toledo 1985, 48-49. The reason for the exchange, initiated by Irenaeus in *Adv. Haer.* III 18,7; 19,1 (SCh 211-366; 374); IV 20,3; 33,4 (SCh 100,634; 810), is echoed in the early fathers. Other references will be found in LADARIA L.F., *Teología del pecado original y de la gracia*, BAC, Madrid 2001³,151.

The Incarnation and the Definition of Humanity

But there is more: has humanity, which was saved in Christ, the Son of God incarnate, had a connection with Christ since the beginning? It is a fact that for centuries humanity's relationship with Christ has been seen more in the framework of redemption and eschatological salvation than that of protology. This is perfectly explained, since it is obvious that the New Testament and the Church's tradition have mainly insisted on this path. It is salvation in Christ that has been and continues to be the primary object of the Church proclamations. But the theology of the past several decades has underscored some aspects in this tradition that show more clearly the relationship of Christ with every human being due to creation itself. The New Testament affirms, first and foremost, that Christ is the image of God (cfr. 2 Cor 4:4; Col 1:15), but it also tells us that humanity is called to reproduce the image of Christ, the heavenly man (cfr. Rom 8:29; 1 Cor 15:49; 2 Cor 3:18). Does this fact give any meaning to the Christian interpretation of Genesis 1:26-27, the creation of humanity in the image and likeness of God? Some fathers of the earlier centuries have understood this to be the case. Above all Irenaeus, for whom only through the incarnation can we understand what humanity being made in the image of God truly means. It was only at the incarnation that the Genesis narrative was fully realized: from the very beginning of creation, the virgin soil from which God formed the body of the first Adam was the figure of Mary, the Virgin from whom the new Adam would be born[19]. With even greater clarity, Tertullian said that in the dust with which God formed Adam, there already existed the idea of Christ, who was to become part of humanity[20]. Christ, who had to be the truest and most complete human being,

---

19 IRENAEUS OF LYONS, *Demonst.* 22 (FP 2,106): «And the image of God is the Son in whose image humans have been made. This is why in recent times it has been manifested to propose that the image was similar to itself»; 32 (123): «From this earth, still virgin, God took dust and formed man, the beginning of the human species. To therefore fulfill this human, the Lord assumed the same bodily disposition, born of a virgin by the will and wisdom of God… so that what, from the start, had been written be fulfilled: man, image and likeness of God». Cfr. also *Adv. Haer.* III 21,10; 22,3 (SCh 211,428-430; 438); V 16,2 (SCh 153,216). The parallel of the virgin earth also appears in HILARY OF POITIERS, *Tract. Myst.* I 2 (SCh 18 bis,76).

20 TERTULLIAN, *De carnis res.* 6 (CCL 2,928): «Quodqumque limus exprimebatur, Christus cogitabatur homo futurus. Id utique quod finxit, ad imaginem Dei fecit illum, scilicet Christi… In limus ille, iam tunc imaginem induens Christi futuri in carne, non tantum Dei opus erat, sed et pignus». The first part of this text is cited in *Gaudium et Spes* 22.

wanted humanity to be made in his image and likeness[21]. With these ideas in mind, the Second Vatican Council was inspired when it has said that the mystery of humanity is only made clear in the mystery of the incarnate Word, and that Christ fully manifests humanity to humanity itself (*Gaudium et Spes* 22).

Catholic theology of the second half of the twentieth century highlighted these and other similar ideas. We must mention Karl Rahner's fruitful intuition when he referred to the possibility of the incarnation as the condition for the possibility of creation. In the incarnation of the Son, the creation of his humanity took place by the very fact of assuming it, so that the humanity of Jesus exists only insofar as it was assumed by the Word. If God can make this creaturely reality totally his, he can express himself in it by assuming it. This divine capacity, which the incarnation demonstrates, finds the possibility of expression in creation; in particular, the human being constitutes the grammar of revelation and the divine self-expression of the incarnation of the Son. Thus, humanity is that which emerges when God wants to be «no-God»[22]. It is not only that salvation comes through the presence of the Son of God in the world, who by his death and resurrection liberated us from sin and death and makes us participants in his divine life; from the beginning, humanity has been thought of by God as the image of his incarnate Son. The Second Vatican Council teaches us that in following Jesus, the «perfect man», we become more human (*Gaudium et Spes* 41; also no. 22).

The union with Jesus to which we are all called is a grace and a gift, not of our own merit. But it is grace that perfects humanity intrinsically, because from the beginning there is no other human vocation than conforming oneself with Christ. Thus, Jesus Christ, the Son of God made man, enters into the Christian definition of humanity from the very beginning and not only in terms of our salvation. «All men are called to this union with Christ, who is the light of the world, from whom we go forth, through whom we live, and toward whom our whole

---

21 TERTULLIAN, *Adv. Prax.* XII 3-4 (Scarpat 170-172): «Cum quibus enim faciebat et quibus faciebat similem? Filio quidem qui erat induiturus hominem, Spiritui vero qui erat sanctificaturus hominem… Erat autem ad cuius imaginem faciebat, ad Filii scicilet, qui homo futurus certior et verior, imaginem suam fecerat dici hominem qui tunc de limo formari habebat, imago veri et similitudo».

22 Cfr. RAHNER K., «Para la teología de la encarnación» in *Escritos de Teología* IV, Madrid 1964, 139-157, esp. 151-153; cfr. also *Grundkurs des Glaubens. Einführung in den Begriff des Christentums*, Freiburg 1976, 220-225; VON BALTHASAR H.U. refers to creation as the grammar of revelation in *Theologik* II, *Wahrheit Gottes*, Einsiedeln 1985, 73.76. Cfr. CORDOVILLA PÉREZ A., *Gramática de la encarnación. La creación en Cristo en la teología de Karl Rahner y Hans Urs von Balthasar*, Universidad Pontificia Comillas, Madrid 2004, 136-139, 451-457.

life strains» (*Lumen Gentium* 3). The incarnation of the Son and all that flows from it implies a faith in a unitary destiny of humanity and a deep connection that unites every human being in a community of origin and destiny in Jesus Christ, through whom we join with God —a unity that will be realized in its entirety only in the future, but of which we already have a first inkling (cfr. *Lumen Gentium* 1;5).

4

The Universal Relevance of the Incarnation and the Theology of Religion
❧

No aspect of Christian theology can bypass the fundamental fact of the incarnation of the Son of God, and certainly not theology of the religions or inter-religious dialogue stemming from it. For a long time, theology has dealt with the salvation of non-Christians, and the main question was how the salvation of Christ could come to those who don't know him and haven't been joined to him by baptism. But together with the uniqueness of the mediation of Christ, the universal reach of this mediation must be affirmed as inseparably bound to the universal saving will of God. And given that human beings don't live any dimension of their lives in isolation, approximately since the time of the Second Vatican Council, it is not only the problem of salvation that holds the attention of theology, but also the significance that other religions may have in terms of this salvation[23]. The problem has thus emerged: is it not underestimating these religions and the stature of their founders to keep on insisting on the exclusive mediation of Christ? Can it and should it still be maintained? Two questions crisscross in the contemporary discussion of these problems: the universal significance of Jesus Christ and the value to be attributed to other religions in the salvation of their followers and in the overall plan of God. Are these incompatible requirements? Indeed, is it not a devaluation or a diminishment of the value of these religions to think that whatever is good in them has to do with Christ, the incarnate Son of God?

Diverse teaching documents of the Catholic Church have attempted to harmonize both extremes of this issue. Beginning with the Second Vatican Council's

---

23 LADARIA L.F., «Du "De vera religione" à l'action universelle de l'Esprit-Saint dans la théologie catholique récente» *in* DORÉ J. (ed.), *Le christianisme vis-à-vis des religions*, Namur 1977, 53-75.

declaration *Nostra Aetate*, as well as other Council documents (in particular, *Lumen Gentium* and *Ad Gentes*), until the encyclical *Redemptoris Missio* and the recent declaration *Dominus Iesus*[24], the uniqueness and universality of the mediation of Christ have been clearly affirmed, while, at the same time, it is argued that this universality does not constitute an obstacle for the union of humanity with God; rather, it is the path to it (cfr. John 14:6)[25]. It cannot be otherwise if we take into account everything we have said previously about the incarnation, death, and resurrection of Jesus and their universal effects. The unprecedented and unique event of God taking on human flesh is a drawing close of the divine, and consequently an incomparable exaltation of the dignity of man. This is an essential Christian truth. Is it licit to reduce the effects of this incarnation to those who believe in Christ while excluding those who without guilt do not know him? Can another hypothetical mediation of salvation give human beings what we Christians affirm that Jesus Christ gives us, he who has saved us through the paschal mystery, and having risen into heaven, continues to intercede for us before the Father (cfr. Rom 8:34; Heb 7:25; 9:24)? If our starting point is the meaning attributed to the incarnation in the New Testament and the tradition of the Church, the universal mediation of Christ cannot be ignored. The Son of God is made man for the salvation of all, and in his incarnation God has made himself known in the fullest sense possible: «he has revealed to mankind *who he is*. This definitive self-revelation of God is the fundamental reason why the Church is missionary by her very nature»[26].

It is precisely this universality of the mystery of Christ that takes his presence beyond the visible frontiers of the Church. We cannot forget the fruitful teaching of the Second Vatican Council on the uniqueness of the mediation of Christ: «the unique mediation of the Redeemer does not exclude but rather gives rise to a manifold cooperation which is but a sharing in this one source» (*Lumen Gentium* 62; also n. 60). This general teaching, formulated by the Council in the context of Mariology, is spoken of similarly in *Redemptoris Missio*: «Although

---

24 In between these two masterful texts we find in 1996 the document *El cristianismo y las religiones*. Cfr. COMISIÓN TEOLÓGICA INTERNACIONAL, *Documentos 1969-1996*, POZO C., S.J. (ed.) I E 4, BAC, Madrid 1998, 557-604.

25 JOHN PAUL II in *Redemptoris Missio* 5 maintained: «Humans cannot enter into communion with God other than through Christ, under the action of the Holy Spirit. This unique and universal mediation, far from being an obstacle to the path towards God is the path established by God himself, and Christ has full awareness of this».

26 JOHN PAUL II, *Redemptoris Missio* 5.

participated forms of mediation of different kinds and degrees are not excluded, they acquire meaning and value only from Christ's own mediation, and they cannot be understood as parallel or complementary to his»[27]. The uniqueness of Christ's mediation receives its meaning if it is contemplated not only as it *excludes* other mediation of similar rank, but also as it *includes* subordinated and participated mediations that receive their value and strength from him. It is in this sense that we must understand what the documents we have referred to say about the value of other religions.

The efforts, including the religious ones, with which humanity has in many ways searched for God, may be considered as evangelical preparation (*Ad Gentes* 3). Whatever is good and true in religions is also evangelical preparation (*Lumen Gentium* 16). Among different peoples and cultures there are elements of truth and grace that, with evangelical preaching, are restored to Christ, their author. Whatever good is found in cultures and rites (a reference to other religions) is not abolished, but healed (*Ad Gentes* 9). The reference to Christ, the author of all good, and to the sowing that recalls the old theology of the seed of the Logos is notable. These ideas are more explicitly mentioned in the same documents: Christians must discover with joy the seed of the Word in the local and religious traditions of different peoples (*Ad Gentes* 11).

In other religions there are holy and true elements, and their teachings do not infrequently (*haud raro*) reflect a ray of the truth that illuminates all of humanity (*Nostra Aetate* 2). Therefore, to discover Christ's presence in other religions is not unfamiliar to the Council's thinking, even though we are also reminded that everything that these religions teach is not always in accordance with what the Church professes (*Nostra Aetate* 2), that the wealth of the diverse peoples should be examined in the light of the Gospel (*Ad Gentes* 11), and that in them there are elements to be healed, elevated, and perfected (*Ad Gentes* 9)[28].

Redemptoris Missio has affirmed that while gifts of all kinds are discovered and valued, especially the spiritual wealth God has given all peoples, we cannot

---

27 JOHN PAUL II, *Redemptoris Missio* 5. The Declaration *Dominus Iesu* 14, expressly relates these two passages. The first one refers to the intra-ecclesial participation in the mediation of Christ, while the second one refers to the extra-ecclesial locus.

28 More or less in conciliar times, RAHNER K., one of the pioneers in acknowledging the positive values of other religions, insisted on the imperfections, including depravities, that can take place in these religions. Cfr. «El cristianismo y las religiones no cristianas» in *Escritos de Teología* v, Taurus, Madrid 1964, 135-156, esp. 141,146 and 150. Cfr. LADARIA L.F., «Karl Rahner: Cristo nelle religioni del mondo» in SANNA I. (ed.), *L'eredità teologica di Karl Rahner*, Rome 2005, 243-269.

separate them from Christ.[29] While it recalls the theme of the seed of the Word, which was present in the documents of Vatican II, the encyclical insists on the presence of the Holy Spirit in peoples, cultures, and religions: «The Spirit's presence and activity affect not only the individuals but also society and history, peoples, cultures and religions». It is Christ resurrected who acts by virtue of his Spirit, who is the one who distributes the seed of the Word to prepare people to mature in Christ[30].

It still affirms that the Spirit is not an alternative to Christ, nor does he fill a void that is sometimes supposed to exist between Christ and the Logos. «Whatever the Spirit brings about in human hearts and in the history of peoples, in cultures and religions serves as a preparation for the Gospel and can only be understood in reference to Christ, the Word who took flesh by the power of the Spirit …»[31]. On the other hand, the Church tries to discover the seed of the Word and the rays of truth in people and in other religious traditions of humanity, hoping to recognize in them signs of the presence of Christ and of the Spirit[32]. There is also a warning that there are, alongside this divine presence in the spiritual traditions of other religions, «gaps, insufficiencies and mistakes»[33]. Obviously, an elementary prudence impedes making positive statements of a global nature on the religious phenomenon in its totality, given its enormous extent and the ambiguities that occasionally go with it[34].

The declaration *Dominus Iesus*, besides recalling some of the main points from previous documents, insists that the various traditions contain and offer religious elements that come from God and are part of what the Spirit sows in the hearts of human beings and in other cultures and religions. Some elements of other religions may serve as a preparation for the Gospel to the degree that

---

29 Cfr. *Redemptoris Missio* 6. In this context the teaching of the Second Vatican Council, *Gaudium et Spes* 22 has kept the following in mind: «Given that "with the incarnation the Son of God has, somehow, become united to all humans" "we ought to maintain *(tenere)* that the Holy Spirit gives everyone the possibility of being associated, in the manner God knows, with the paschal mystery". The divine design is "to recapitulate in Christ all things, those in heaven and those on earth"» (Eph 1:10).

30 JOHN PAUL II, *Redemptoris Missio* 28. Cfr. *Redemptor hominis* 11.

31 JOHN PAUL II, *Redemptoris Missio* 29.

32 Cfr. JOHN PAUL II, *Redemptoris Missio* 56.

33 JOHN PAUL II, *Redemptoris Missio* 55. The words in quotes come from Paul VI at the opening of Session II of the Second Vatican Council. The Declaration *Dominus Iesu* 21 indicates, in reference to *Redemptoris Missio* 55, that some elements of other religions may be an obstacle to eternal salvation. Texts of *Dominus Iesu* and *Redemptoris Missio*, in general, do not exactly coincide.

34 Cfr. the document *El cristianismo y las otras religiones* 87, published by the COMISIÓN TEOLÓGICA INTERNACIONAL, *Documentos 1969-1996*, POZO C., S.J. (ed.), BAC, Madrid 1998, 591.

they are paths or pedagogy for people to open their hearts to the action of God[35]. An explicit mention is made of the sacred books of other religions: «The sacred books of other religions, which in actual fact direct and nourish the existence of their followers, receive from the mystery of Christ the elements of goodness and grace which they contain»[36].

If we have lingered on these texts, it is to demonstrate how frequently the explicit mention of Christ appears when it is a question of recognizing the existence of spiritual riches and elements of grace in diverse religions. Christian theology of religions begins with the universal significance of Christ and his incarnation. Otherwise, the universal significance and the unique mediation attested to by the New Testament and the tradition of the Church are compromised. To speak of elements of grace, of rays of truth, and of the seed of the Word means to speak of Christ, in whom is manifested the grace of God (cfr. Tit 2:11), who is the true light that illuminates every human being (cfr. John 1:9), who is truth (cfr. John 14:6), and who is the only Word in which God has made himself totally known to humanity. If the universal saving will of God and the uniqueness of Christ's mediation are to be maintained as the New Testament presents them, the only possible answer is to contemplate a mysterious, although no less real, presence of Christ, the incarnate Son of God. The tradition of the Church offers a broad base to affirm this and, directly or indirectly, many of these elements have been given new value in recent times.

Therefore, when we propose, from a Christian perspective, the theology of religions, we cannot forget that the first theological question at hand is that of the universal significance of the incarnation, for us and for our salvation—a salvation realized first and foremost in the paschal mystery. This maintains, in all their power, the scandal of the cross (cfr. 1 Cor 1:17, 23; Gal 6:14) and the scandal of the incarnation[37].

---

35 Cfr. *Dominus Iesus* 21.
36 *Dominus Iesus* 8.
37 TERTULLIAN, *De carne Christi* 5,1-8 (CCL 2,880-882): «What is there more unworthy of God or what is that of which he should be more ashamed? To be born or to die? To bear flesh or to bear the cross? To be circumcised or to be crucified? To be laid in a crib or to be laid in a tomb?… Do not take away the only hope in the whole world. Why eliminate the necessary vengeance of faith? What is shameful for God benefits me: I am saved if I am not to be confused because of my Lord… The Son of God was crucified. I am not ashamed because one must be ashamed. He died as Son of God; it is believable because it is unbelievable… But how are these things true in Christ, if Christ himself was not true, if he did not truly have in himself what could be hung on the cross, dead, put to rest and resurrected… This, the reality of his dual substance, showed him as man and God, born and unborn, carnal and spiritual, weak and super strong, dying and alive… Why do you slash Christ in half with lies? He, as a whole, was true».

Both are mutually implied. The commitment of God to humanity in the incarnation is such that the Son, from the moment of his incarnation until his ascension into heaven, exists only in the humanity he has assumed and to which he has become united hypostatically. «Quod semel Adsumpsit adsumpsit nunquam dimisit» is an axiom implicit in the Christology and soteriology of the early centuries, vis-à-vis gnostic trends that despised the flesh of the Lord[38].

In this same line of thought, we have to place the known statements of Saint Leo the Great about Christ's actions according to his dual nature but in the deep unity of his person, so that after the incarnation no divine actions are realized without his humanity, nor human deeds without his divinity[39]. This also easily explains why the declaration *Dominus Iesus* considers in manifest contrast with Christian faith the thesis that «to justify the universality of Christian salvation as well as the fact of religious pluralism, it has been proposed that there is an economy of the eternal Word that is valid also outside the Church and is unrelated to her, in addition to an economy of the incarnate Word. The first would have a greater universal value than the second, which is limited to Christians, though God's presence would be fuller in the second»[40]. This proposed solution to the problem clashes with the obvious barrier of the clear statements in the New Testament and the entire tradition of the Church about the unique mediation of Christ and the salvation that comes to us through his death and resurrection —in other words, about the universal value of the work of salvation conducted by and through the humanity of Jesus. But, on the other hand, perhaps in a less visible fashion, it supposes a deficient understanding of the incarnation of the Son, as if he could behave for the salvation of humanity in such a way that his own humanity could be placed in parenthesis. This is not the Christian conception of the incarnation of the Word. Christ has irrevocably assumed human nature, and this is the hope of salvation for humanity as a whole[41].

---

38 Cfr. GONZÁLEZ DE CARDEDAL O., *Cristología*, BAC, Madrid 2005, 546; ORBE A., *En torno a la encarnación*, Aldecoa, Burgos 1985, 205-219.

39 Cfr. DH 294; 317-318.

40 *Dominus Iesus* 9; also cfr. *no.* 10.

41 *Dominus Iesus*, 10: «It is not compatible with the Doctrine of the Church the theory which attributes to the Word as such a salvific activity which would take place at "the margins" and "beyond" the humanity of Jesus Christ, also after incarnation». Cfr. the document *El cristianismo y las otras religiones* 39 published by the COMISIÓN TEOLÓGICA INTERNACIONAL: «Neither a limitation of the saving will of God, nor the admission of parallel mediations to that of Jesus, nor an attribution of this universal mediation to the Logos unidentified with Jesus become compatible with the message of the New Testament».

To think of a saving presence of the eternal Word in which his humanity somehow remains in parenthesis for those living outside the visible frontiers of Christianity is an attempt to diminish or weaken the divine presence in the world. Then we do not have «God with us» in the same radical way that the New Testament presents it (cfr. Matt 1:23); we do not have the Word who joins every human being in his incarnation. The Christian theology of religions should acknowledge the mysterious presence of Christ, the incarnate Son of God, in whatever elements of truth, grace, and assistance toward salvation that may be found in them. Otherwise, an illegitimate separation in Christ would be introduced[42]. Precisely because of trying to maintain the distinction between his two natures, there arises a risk of establishing between them a separation, equally contrary to the Chalcedonian definition, and of forgetting the meaning and scope of the unity of the person of Christ, which is one and the same in both natures.

5

The Incarnation and the Gift of the Spirit

In the Christian theology of religions and of inter-religious dialogue, the theme of the action of the Holy Spirit cannot be left aside. In the texts we have previously mentioned briefly, it has appeared frequently. The universal meaning of Christ and his unique mediation are necessarily related to the action of the *Holy Spirit*, which knows no frontiers. Indeed, although the Spirit may manifest himself in a particular way in the Church and its members, his presence and the effects of it are *universal, without limits in space and time.* If he exercises a peculiar action in the body of Christ, the Church, we cannot separate from it the universal action he realizes while giving to the world the seed of the Word, planting and developing his different gifts among all peoples[43]. «Because the spirit of the Lord has filled the world» (Wis 1:7), and the same Spirit is compared to the wind blowing where it wishes without us knowing where it comes from or is going (cfr. John 3:8). Is this action of the Spirit broader than that of Christ? Is it possible to think of a presence of the Spirit among non-Christian religions and their followers that is the gift of the Son «as such» and not the gift of Pentecost, of Jesus

---

42 *Redemptoris Missio* 6: «It is contrary to Christian faith to introduce any separation between the Word and Jesus Christ».

43 Cfr. *Redemptoris Missio* 28-29.

Christ resurrected and risen into heaven? In other words, is the presence of the Spirit more universal than that of Jesus incarnate, dead and risen?

The deep bond between the life of Christ and the Spirit has been underscored from ancient times[44]. The Spirit is present from the moment of the incarnation of Jesus (cfr. Matt 1:18-20; Luke 1:35). In the fourth Gospel there is the testimony of John the Baptist, who says he has seen the Spirit descend upon Jesus and remain with him (cfr. John 1:32-34). The motive of this permanence is new in relation to the narratives of the baptism in the synoptics, in which the descent of the Spirit upon Jesus is also an essential element (cfr. Mark 1:9-11). Other New Testament passages refer to this moment as the anointing of Jesus (cfr. Luke 4:18; Acts 10:38). Jesus offers himself to the Father in his passion through an eternal Spirit (cfr. Heb 9:14) and was declared to be the Son of God with power according to the Spirit of holiness by his resurrection from the dead (cfr. Rom 1:4). The outpouring of the Spirit by the risen Lord, glorified at the right hand of the Father, shows that the messianic age prophesied since ancient times has finally arrived (cfr. Acts 2:16). In the ancient tradition of the Church, the presence of the Spirit in Jesus during his mortal life and the outpouring of the Holy Spirit after the resurrection have been seen in an intimate relationship. For Justin, with the coming of Christ the gift of prophecy ceased to exist among the Jews, as a new outpouring of the Spirit was to have Jesus as its only principle[45]. And for Irenaeus of Lyons, the Spirit came at the Jordan upon the incarnate Son of God so that we would be saved through receiving the abundance of his anointing[46].

It is, therefore, perfectly coherent with the New Testament, and it fully corresponds to the tradition of the Church, to affirm that the mystery of the incarnate Word is the place of the Holy Spirit's presence in the world and the beginning of

---

44 Cfr. for example BASIL THE GREAT, *De Spiritu sancto,* 16,39 (SCh 17 bis,386): «The salvation plan for all humans… who can doubt it is fulfilled with the grace of the Holy Spirit?… First, he was in the very flesh of the Lord, turned into unction and inseparably, as it is written: "He on whom you see the Spirit descend and remain, is the one who baptizes with the Holy Spirit" (John 1:33; Luke 3:22). And: "God anointed Jesus of Nazareth with the Holy Spirit" (Acts 10:38). And after all, the activity of Christ was carried out in the presence of the Holy Spirit».

45 Cfr. *Dial. Tryph.* 87, 3-6 (PTS 47,222).

46 Cfr. IRENAEUS OF LYONS, *Adv. Haer.* III 9,3 (SCh 211,112): «Secundum id quod Verbum Dei homo erat ex radice Iesse et filius Abrahae, secundum hoc requiescebat Spiritus Dei super eum et unguebatur et evangelizandum humilibus… Spiritus ergo Dei descendit in eum, eius qui per prophetas promiserat uncturum se eum, ut de abundantia unctionis sius nos percipientes salvaremur». ATHANASIUS OF ALEXANDRIA, *Contra Arianos* I 47 (PG 26,109): «it is not the Logos, inasmuch as it is Logos and Wisdom, who is anointed with the Holy Spirit he gives, but it is the assumed flesh that is anointed in him and by him, so that the sanctification which has come onto the Lord as man may be passed on to human beings».

his outpouring on humanity[47]. It is the place of his presence because it is in Christ that the Spirit rests and remains, because in his humanity he becomes accustomed to dwelling among humanity[48]. Christ is the principle of his outpouring once glorified (cfr. John 7:39), because the Spirit now fully penetrates his humanity, which is no longer subject to death, and by the same Spirit we can become participants in the divine life that Christ now fully possesses. Christ's mission in the world, accomplished by his incarnation, and the Holy Spirit's mission do not simply juxtapose the other, but rather imply each one in the other. The Spirit is communicated to us as a gift of the resurrected Christ. Therefore, he is called the Spirit of Christ, of Jesus, of Jesus Christ (cfr. Rom 8:9; 1 Pet 1:11; Acts 16:7; Phil 1:19; Gal 4:6). The Spirit bursts from his glorified humanity[49]. The New Testament does not recognize a gift of the Holy Spirit that is not linked to the resurrection of Jesus and not oriented to the consummation of his saving work.

The Spirit makes Christ's work universal, internal, and actual[50]. His action is not located outside of or as an alternative to that of Christ. There is only one economy of salvation, which has its origin in the initiative of the Father and its center in the mystery of the life, death, and resurrection of Christ, whose effects reach to the ends of the earth, thanks to the action of the Spirit, who is the gift of both the Father and of the resurrected Christ Jesus.

The glorified humanity of Christ fills the universe. It does not limit nor is it an obstacle to the universal presence of the Spirit, as this spiritualized and divinized humanity surpasses all limitations of time and space. Full of the Spirit, it becomes, through the action of the Spirit itself, a «life-giving spirit» (1 Cor 15:45). The glorious humanity of the Lord is penetrated by the Spirit. From this humanity the influx and action of the Spirit reaches all human beings as the Spirit of the resurrected one. If the Spirit did not bear the stamp of the glorified humanity of the Lord, he would not be able to conform us with Christ. Is there any path of salvation other than following Christ (to the degree that it is possible, according to each person's situation), and is there any other content of salvation itself but conformity with Christ and sharing in his life? This is another

---

47   Cfr. *Dominus Iesus* 12.
48   Cfr. IRENAEUS OF LYONS, *Adv. Haer.* III 17,1 (SCh 211,330).
49   IRENAEUS OF LYONS, *Adv. Haer.* III 24,1 (SCh 211,472): «deposita est [in Ecclesia] communicatio Christi, id est Spiritus Sanctus». Ibid., (474): «…neque percipiunt de corpore Christi procedentem nitidissimum fontem…».
50   Cfr. GONZÁLEZ DE CARDEDAL O., *Dios*, Salamanca 2004, 52.

point that we must keep in mind when considering the value of the incarnation in the context of the theology of religions.

The Configuration with the Glorified Christ: Fullness for All Humanity

Indeed, the New Testament often presents salvation as a participation in the life of the glorified humanity of Jesus (cfr. John 14:1-3; 17:24-26; Rom 8:16-17, 29; 1 Cor 15:45-49; Eph 1:3-14; Col 3:1-4). The tradition of the Church has frequently underscored that whenever the New Testament mentions the glorification of Christ, his exaltation, and so forth, it is referring to his human nature, since in his divine nature he cannot grow or perfect himself[51]. Given this distinction, whatever is said about the perfection of his human condition may also be said of ours as well by virtue of the inclusion of all humanity in him, to which we have previously referred[52]. The content of our salvation is essentially linked, therefore, to the fullness of the divine life that Jesus received in his humanity. We are all called to place ourselves within the body of the Church, which will not reach its fullness until the whole human race and the entire universe has been completely renewed[53]. Christian faith begins with the premise of the unity of humanity as a whole because of its origins in Adam, and above all, because of its destiny in Christ.

It is inconceivable that salvation, as it is presented in the New Testament, is only for Christians and not for those who do not know Christ. Theologically, it is unthinkable that salvation for non-Christians assumes different characteristics[54], especially if the mystery of Christ transcends the limits of space and time

51 Cfr. LEO THE GREAT, *Letter Promississe me memini* (DH 318); HILARY OF POITIERS, *De Trinitate* III 16; XI 18-19 (CCL 62,87-88; 62A,547-550).
52 Cfr. ATHANASIUS OF ALEXANDRIA, *De incarnatione Verbi et contra Arianos* 12 (PG 26,1004): «Everything that in the Scriptures says Jesus has received, it says it because of his body, who is first in the Church ... In the first place, the Lord has resurrected his own body and has exalted it in himself. Later, he has resurrected all members, to give them, as God, all that he has received as man»; ibid., 21 (1021): «When Peter says: "Therefore, let the whole house of Israel know for certain that God has made him both Lord and Messiah, this Jesus whom you crucified" (Acts 2:36), it is not of divinity that he says Jesus is constituted Lord and Christ, but of his humanity, who is the whole Church». The Church is related to this whole humanity, because it has been assumed by the Son in his incarnation.
53 Cfr. *Lumen Gentium* 48.
54 Cfr. Document *El cristianismo y las religiones*, 49 (published by the COMISIÓN TEOLÓGICA INTERNACIONAL, *op.cit.*, 576): «Jesus, being the sole Mediator fulfilling the saving design of the only God

and achieves the unity of the human family[55]. If this is so, can we conceive of different paths other that of Christ to reach the one and only goal, which is Christ himself? This solution would ignore the intimate bond between the mediator of salvation and salvation itself. Who but Jesus himself, through his Spirit, is able to communicate to us the fullness of the divine life that he enjoys in his glorified humanity? Thus, Christ's humanity has an eternal significance for our relationship with God[56].

7

Open reflections: the Universal Presence of the Spirit of Christ

⌘

The universal presence of the Spirit of Christ is the principle that allows for a positive assessment of the many elements of other religions. To conceive of complements to the revelation of Christ, in whom the fullness of divinity dwells (cfr. Col 2:9), or parallel paths of salvation that do not go by way of the incarnate, dead, and risen Jesus, is, in reality, to forget the great mystery of Christ, who became a human being for all humanity. To accept this line of thought would mean not giving the due weight and value to the presence of God among human beings, and thus the presence of God would not really affect the whole human race.

According to Christian theology, the incarnation of the Son of God, his death, and his resurrection are the supreme manifestations of the divine presence in the world, and are thus saving. To think that this presence, through paths known to God, may be alive and operating in other religions by virtue of the Spirit of Jesus Christ does not mean that they are any less esteemed. The Church is called to discover, through inter-religious dialogue, the seed of the Word and the rays of truth found in the diverse religious traditions of humanity, and to discover in them signs of the presence of Christ and of the action of the Spirit[57]. In this way, the Church is enriched, for it can never have full consciousness of the

---

the Father, salvation for all humans is unique and the same one: the full configuration with Jesus and the communion with him in the participation of his divine Sonship».

55 Cfr. *Dominus Iesus* 23.

56 Cfr. the classic and widely accepted articles of RAHNER K. about Christ's humanity: «Eterna significación de la humanidad de Jesús para nuestra relación con Dios» in *Escritos de Teología* III, Madrid 1967, 47-59; and also ALFARO J., «Cristo glorioso, revelador del Padre» in *Cristología y antropología. Temas teológicos actuales,* Madrid 1973, 141-182.

57 Cfr. *Redemptoris Missio* 56; cfr. also no. 29.

greatness of the mystery of Christ in the full variety of its manifestations. The mystery of Christ, which can only be fully experienced in the Church, makes itself present throughout the earth. The Church is, as the body of Christ, the privileged place of the presence of the Spirit[58], in whom the fullness of the means of salvation is enjoyed. But the same Spirit offers all human beings the possibility of being in contact, in ways known only to God, with the paschal mystery[59]. The mystery of God becoming a human being to save humanity, which is the climax and fullness of revelation, is at the center of the Christian message. This must always be remembered when the issue of assessing the phenomenon of the religious tradition of humanity arises.

«Solus enim passurus pro omnibus omnium peccata solvebat, nec socium admittit quidquid universitati praestatur ab uno» (He alone was to suffer for all and redeem the sins of all, and what is given to all by only one, does not allow for a companion)[60]. Jesus is the sole redeemer, and although joined to all human beings, who are indeed his companions, he alone possesses the unity of redemptive action. He is the only one who, suffering for all, gives life and salvation to the whole human race. The Son, the firstborn of the Father, who became a human being for us, is the only savior. Through him all the properties of salvation come to humanity, and only from him can they come to us. Only in him can humanity attain union with God; no one goes to the Father except through Jesus (John 14:5-6). To believe that human fullness can come through paths other than the Word who has become our *brother* is to have a low esteem for the salvation of all humankind[61].

---

58 IRENAEUS OF LYONS, *Adversus Haereses* III 24,1 (SCh 211,474): «Where the Spirit of the Lord is, there the Church is, and where the Church is, there the Spirit of the Lord is and all of his grace». It is not enough to suggest here the ecclesiological dimension of this universal relevance of the salvation of Christ, which cannot be separated from his body, which is a sacrament, that is, a sign and instrument of the union of humanity with God realized only in Christ. *Redemptoris Missio* 10: «For them [who do not know Christ] the salvation of Christ is accessible by virtue of a grace that, although it has a mysterious relationship with the Church, does not formally introduce them to her, but rather it enlightens them in an adequate manner on their inner and environmental situation. This grace comes from Christ. It is fruit of his sacrifice and is communicated by the Holy Spirit».

59 Cfr. *Gaudium et Spes* 22.

60 HILARY OF POITIERS, *In Mt.* 14,16 (SCh 258,30).

61 CLEMENT OF ALEXANDRIA, *Second Letter* I 1-2 (FP 3,177): «It is necessary not to have low esteem regarding our salvation. If we do have low esteem for it, likewise, we will hope to attain little».

Christianity and the Universality of Salvation

1

Guidelines from the Second Vatican Council

℘

This theme, which was precisely developed in the commemorative context of the ending of the Second Vatican Council, certainly corresponds to the deep spirit that animated the Council to transmit a message of hope to all humanity[1]. The pastoral constitution *Gaudium et Spes* says at its very beginning:

> Therefore, the council focuses its attention on the world of men, the whole human family along with the sum of those realities in the midst of which it lives; that world which is the theater of man's history, and the heir of his energies, his tragedies and his triumphs; that world which the Christian sees as created and sustained by its Maker's love, fallen indeed into the bondage of sin, yet emancipated now by Christ, who was crucified and rose again to break the strangle hold of personified evil, so that the world might be fashioned anew according to God's design and reach its fulfillment[2].

The horizon on which the concern for the human race is placed is that of the good news of salvation that the Church has received and is called to communicate to all (*Gaudium et Spes* 1;3). Looking within and outside of the Church, gazing on high, and contemplating the world around us, all these dimensions are harmonized in the conviction that Christ is not indifferent toward humanity, and that his Church, in Christ himself, is like a sacrament, that is, a sign and instrument of union with God and of the union of the whole human species (*Lumen Gentium* 1; *Gaudium et Spes* 42). These two elements are deeply intertwined; they imply and condition each other. It is not God's wish to save human beings individually or in an isolated way; he wants to bring humanity together as a people (*Lumen Gentium* 9), to call believers to the Church (*Lumen Gentium* 2), and to gather them in unity—a unity in which no one can think of himself or herself as being excluded: «All people are called to this union with Christ, who is the light of the world, from whom we go forth, through whom we live, and toward whom our whole life strains» (*Lumen Gentium* 3).

---

1 For more on this theme cfr. LADARIA L.F., «El cristianismo y la universalidad de la salvación» in *Estudios Eclesiásticos* 81 (2006) 353-381.
2 *Gaudium et Spes* 2.

Without reviewing all of the texts in which the Council reflects on the universality of Christ's salvation, we cannot fail to mention the instruction to the people of God concerning those who have not yet received the Gospel, as it is presented in *Lumen Gentium*, in the few lines below:

> Nor does Divine Providence deny the helps necessary for salvation to those who, without blame on their part, have not yet arrived at an explicit knowledge of God and with his grace strive to live a good life. Whatever good or truth is found amongst them is looked upon by the Church as a preparation for the Gospel. She knows that it is given by him who enlightens all men so that they may finally have life[3].

And, while underlining the missionary character of the Church, the same constitution adds:

> [The Church] through her work, whatever good is in the minds and hearts of men, whatever good lies latent in the religious practices and cultures of diverse peoples, is not only saved from destruction but is also cleansed *(sanetur)*, raised up *(elevetur)* and perfected *(consummetur)* unto the glory of God, the confusion of the devil and the happiness of man ... In this way the Church both prays and labors in order that the entire world may become the people of God, the Body of the Lord and the temple of the Holy Spirit, and that in Christ, the Head of all, all honor and glory may be rendered to the Creator and Father of the Universe[4].

Indeed, the same vocabulary used in *Lumen Gentium* is found in the decree *Ad Gentes:*

> But whatever truth and grace are to be found among the nations, as a sort of secret presence of God, he frees from all taint of evil and restores to Christ its maker ... And so, whatever good is found to be sown in the hearts and minds of men, or in the rites and cultures peculiar to various peoples, not only is not lost, but is healed, uplifted, and perfected *(sanatur, elevatur et consummatur)* for the glory of God, the shame of the devil, and the bliss of men[5].

---

3 *Lumen Gentium* 16.
4 *Lumen Gentium* 17.
5 *Ad Gentes* 9.

With a perspective that is still more directly Christological, *Gaudium et Spes* deals with the question of the universality of salvation in a very frequently cited passage:

> All this [the paschal mystery and being conformed to the death Christ] holds true not only for Christians, but for all men of *good will* in whose hearts grace works in an unseen way. For, since Christ died for all men, and since the ultimate vocation of man is in fact one and divine, we ought to believe that the Holy Spirit in a manner known only to God offers to every man the possibility of being associated with this paschal mystery[6].

Additionally, *Lumen Gentium* insists repeatedly on the unique mediation of Christ (cfr. *Lumen Gentium* 8; 14; 49; 60; 62; *Ad Gentes* 7). The declaration *Nostra Aetate,* for its part, insists from the beginning on the unique origin and the unique destiny of humanity: «One is the community of all peoples, one their origin, for God made the whole human race to live over the face of the earth (cfr. Acts 17:26). One also is their final goal, God. His providence, his manifestations of goodness, his saving design extend to all men» (*Nostra Aetate* 1). This universal plan of salvation and the recognition of the presence of holy and true elements in other religions of the world cannot be considered separately:

> The Catholic Church rejects nothing that is true and holy in these religions. She regards with sincere reverence those ways of conduct and of life, those precepts and teachings which, though differing in many aspects from the ones she holds and sets forth, nonetheless often reflect a ray of that truth which enlightens all men. Indeed, she proclaims, and ever must proclaim Christ *the way, the truth, and the life* (John 14:6), in

---

6 *Gaudium et Spes* 22. There are other references to the unique and divine vocation of humanity and to the unity of the human species in *Gaudium et Spes* 24: «Omnes enim creati ad imaginem Dei, qui fecit *ex uno omne genus hominem inhabitare super universam faciem terrae* (Acts 17:26) ad unum eumdemque finem, id est ad Deum ipsum, vocantur»; *Gaudium et Spes* 29: «Cum omnes homines, anima rationali pollentes et ad imaginem Dei creata, eamdem naturam eamdemque originem habeant, cumque, a Christo redempti, eadem vocatione et destinatione divina fruantur…»; *Gaudium et Spes* 92: «Cum Deus Pater principium omnium exsistet et finis, omnes ut fratres simus vocamur». In these conciliar statements, motives for the unity of the human species, the creation of all humanity in the image and likeness of God, and our ultimate destiny, which is God himself, are combined. Without a doubt, the universality of the design of salvation is at the base of all these passages.

whom men may find the fullness of religious life, in whom God has reconciled all things to himself (cfr. 2 Cor 5:18-19)[7].

2

Developments in Recent Theology on the Universality of Salvation

*

There is no difficulty for the majority of contemporary Christians in accepting the perspective of universal salvation spoken of by the Council, which frequently and explicitly cited several significant New Testament statements: «This is right and acceptable in the sight of God our Savior, who desires everyone to be saved and to come to the knowledge of the truth. For there is one God; there is also one mediator between God and humankind, Christ Jesus, himself human, who gave himself a ransom for all -this was attested at the right time ...» (1 Tim 2:3-6). In post-conciliar theology, it is not surprising to find that universal salvation has gained a special relevance. There are many motives involved: strictly theological ones: the image and notion of God's love that Christianity professes; Christological ones: the universal significance of Christ's redemptive work; and, as a consequence of them, anthropological ones: human beings in the image of God with our unique and supernatural destiny; and finally, eschatological ones: the ultimate realization of the plan of salvation.

To quote one illustrious example among many, in the last volume of his *Theo-Drama*, dedicated precisely to the «final act», Hans Urs von Balthasar, when speaking of the mystery of eternal damnation, offers a statement that is inevitably food for thought:

> While the *gloria Dei* remains assured in any case, both if he saves or condemns, the problem does not become acute. But when the purpose of creation is linked in the closest manner to Trinitarian life, then the problem seems unavoidable. Here one must be aware of the limits of human speculation (we are speaking about «hope of universal redemption» as the most extreme attainable horizon) but one does not have to remain behind in the audacity of this hope, where the issue of the fate of demons stays excluded as insoluble for the *theologia viatorum*[8].

---

7 *Nostra Aetate* 2.
8 VON BALTHASAR H.U., *Teodramática 5. El último acto*, Madrid 1997, 490 (the German original was published in 1983). MARTELET G., *L'au-delà retrouvé. Christologie des fins derniers*, Paris 1975, 188:

Let us also leave aside the thorny question of demons[9] and focus on the destiny of humanity, whose fate has been shared by the Son of God, made one with us, whom God, the creator and artisan of the universe, sent into the world. The Letter to Diognetus reads:

> He sent him in gentleness and meekness as a king sent his son who is king; as a God he was sent to us, as man to men he sent him, to save us he sent him; to persuade, not do violence, for in God there is no violence. He sent him to call, not to punish; he sent him, in sum, to love, not to judge. He would send him one day as judge, and who, then, will resist his coming?[10].

Salvation and judgment, mercy and justice —this is the dilemma in which we are caught, which can be found in the New Testament. We may recall the especially significant passage of Matt 25:31-46, among others. Both extremes will have to be maintained while always bearing in mind that it is salvation, not judgment or punishment, that is the sole purpose of the sending of the Son into the world, in which the Father's love for us has been manifested: «For God so loved the world that he gave his only Son, so that everyone who believes in him may not perish but may have eternal life. Indeed, God did not send the Son into the world to condemn the world, but in order that the world might be saved through him» (John 3:16-17; cfr. 1 John 4:9-10). Only salvation is the goal of Jesus' coming into the world, and in this sense von Balthasar is right when he says that the glory of God makes the problem of damnation an acute one, although for each of us the possibility of rejecting salvation that is offered to us remains very real. But this does not mean that God remains «indifferent» toward us. God has personally committed himself to our salvation, so much so that his glory may be dimmed

---

«Il est divinement impossible que Dieu lui-même puisse coopérer le moins du monde à cette aberration, et surtout para en vue de retrouver, par la victoire de sa justice, la gloire de son amour trahi, comme on l'a trop souvent prétendu».

9 RAHNER K., «Principios teológicos de la hermenéutica de las declaraciones escatológicas» in *Escritos de Teología IV*, Taurus, Madrid 1964, 411-439, 431: «It would be false to validate here the fate of demons. If so, then, it would have to be proven that their salvific situation and ours is the same and that diversity of being lacks importance for our question, which, indeed, is not possible». It is obvious that Karl Rahner refers to the incarnation of the Son, which determines the soteriological situation of the angels as well as humanity. Irenaeus of Lyons with his famous Christological-anthropological formula, was already aware of the problem: «supergrediens angelos» in *Adv. Haer.* V 33,6. Cfr. ORBE A., *Teología de San Ireneo III*, Madrid-Toledo 1988, 632-665; and ORBE A., «Supergrediens Angelos (Saint Irenaeus, *Adv. Haer.* V 33,6)» in *Gregorianum* 54 (1973) 5-59.

10 *To Diognetus* VII 4 (BAC 65, 853).

if some do not attain it. Precisely because of this, some of the leading theologians of the twentieth century have insisted on the possibility of «hope for all». In 1960, still at the time of the preparation of the Second Vatican Council, Karl Rahner published his important article *Theological Principles on the Hermeneutics of the Eschatological Declarations*[11]. In this thesis he broaches the question that we are now addressing:

> Eschatology proceeds, in its content and certitude, from the affirmation of the saving work of God in his grace towards contemporary man, and in this affirmation it has its norm. From there it follows that the eschatology of salvation and that of reprobation are not at the same level ... Christian eschatology, therefore, is not the *symmetric* extension of a two-path doctrine [of salvation and damnation] leading toward those two final goals, (a concept more in tune with the Old Testament than Christian), but rather in its core, it is only the affirmation about the grace of Christ conquering and perfecting the world, although surely in such a way that the mystery of God regarding the individual man while he is still a pilgrim remains hidden[12].

The underscoring of the saving character of Christian eschatology goes along with the explicit exclusion of the *apokatastasis* and the observation that the urgency of this question is not realized when making a general theoretical exposition of it, but when one thinks about it, saying, «I can become lost; I hope to be saved»[13]. Catholic dogma is based on the idea that history in its totality ends with the definite victory of God in his grace, which has already triumphed definitively in Christ; the conclusion of the world is the fullness of the resurrection of Christ, which is equivalent to the resurrection of the flesh and the glorification of the world[14]. Christ's victory is assured, even if the participation of each of us in it may not be.

---

11 Cfr. footnote 9. As noted on previous chapters, this reproduces the text of a conference that took place in Bonn, Germany, in 1960.
12 RAHNER K., «Principios teológicos de la hermenéutica de las declaraciones escatológicas» *in Escritos de Teología IV*, Taurus, Madrid 1964, 431-432. Cfr. also RAHNER K., *Grundkurs des Glaubens. Einführung in den Begriff des Christentums*, Freiburg 1976, 110; 425-426.
13 Cfr. RAHNER K., «Principios teológicos de la hermenéutica de las declaraciones escatológicas» *in Escritos de Teología IV*, 431-432.
14 RAHNER K., «Principios teológicos de la hermenéutica de las declaraciones escatológicas» *in Escritos de Teología IV*, 436. And *Grundkurs des Glaubens*, 426: «The opening to a total freedom of men until a possible perdition is found together with the teaching that the world and the history of the world jointly, in fact, end up in the eternal life of God».

Many years later, perhaps in a more explicit way, Hans Urs von Balthasar further developed this theme[15]. The hope for universal salvation is not only a possibility; it becomes a pressing necessity, keeping in mind that Christian hope deals with God's great saving actions that embrace the whole of creation and have to do with the destiny of all humanity, whose fullness we still await. Inasmuch as each of us belongs to this humanity, this hope refers to you, me, and everyone around us[16]. In fact, the salvation we hope for has to be the culmination of the work of Christ, of the divine plan to recapitulate all things in him, both in heaven and on earth (cfr. Eph 1:10). Texts that speak of this «whole» abound in the New Testament (cfr. Eph 1:10; Col 1:20; Phil 2:10-11; Rom 5:12-21; John 17:2)[17]. Von Balthasar, with his usual insight noted that John's Gospel focused on the idea of judgment and its crisis (*krisis*); the following passage captures this perspective: «and I, when I am lifted up from the earth, will draw all people to myself» (John 12:32)[18]. Can we or should we exclude someone from the universal attraction of the crucified Lord? Would anyone be able to resist the attraction of this powerful magnet? It is at least worthwhile to propose the question.

On the other hand, only within the scope of this totality, of the fullness of God's saving plan realized in Christ, does the fulfillment and the salvation of each of us make sense. It is only the realization of the divine project and its fullness in Christ that assures our salvation. Christ's victory, his kingdom, and the submission of everything to him (cfr. 1 Cor 15:25-27) guarantee the salvation of humanity.

---

15 Toward the end of his life, Hans Urs Von Balthasar wrote two brief books on this question as an answer to debates, provoked by previous publications on this matter: *Was dürfen wir hoffen?* Einsiedeln, 1986, and *Kleiner Diskurs über die Hölle*, Einsiedeln 1987. I will use the third revised and extended edition: *Kleiner Diskurs über die Hölle. Apokatastasis*, Einsiedeln 1999. On the issue as a whole, cfr. NANDKISORE R., *Hoffnung auf Erlösung. Die Eschatologie im Werk Hans Urs von Balthasar*, Roma 1977.

16 VON BALTHASAR H.U., *Kleiner Diskurs über die Hölle. Apokatastasis*, 11-12. Von Balthasar cites in this context: DANIÉLOU J., *Essai sur le mystère de l'histoire*, Paris 1953, 340.

17 Cfr. VON BALTHASAR H.U., *Kleiner Diskurs*, 31-33. In the same context, Von Balthasar refers to distinctions between the antecedent will of God, which wants everyone to be saved, and the consequent one, which wants some to be damned because of the demands of his justice. Cfr. THOMAS AQUINAS, *STh* I 19,6, ad 1: «Deus antecedenter vult omnes homines salvari; sed consequenter vult quosdam damnari, secundum exigentiam suae iustitiae». This view was common among early Church fathers. Cfr. for example, JOHN CHRYSOSTOM, *In Ep. ad Eph. Hom.* I 2 (PG 62,15); JOHN OF DAMASCUS, *De fide ortodoxa* II 29,14 (PG 94,969). In the cited works, there is broad documentation on the problem of harmonizing mercy and bounty with justice, and the conclusions that, historically, this apparent contradiction has nourished. It is not worth dealing with this now. Hope is the practical solution for this problem with no theoretical resolution. Cfr. VON BALTHASAR H.U., *Was dürfen wir hoffen?*, 127.

18 Cfr. VON BALTHASAR H.U., *Was dürfen wir hoffen?*, 32-33.

A particular perspective of hope is not possible, for it would lock us up as individuals and prevent our access to the essential ecclesial dimension of Christian life, which we cannot leave aside when dealing with eschatological hope. The fullness of the body of Christ is the fullness of Christ himself, who did not want to exist without us. Christological considerations should have a certain priority over merely anthropological ones when dealing with Christian eschatology. Jesus is the ultimate and definitive human being (*novissimus Adam*), and only in light of his person, of this Ultimate One, does it make any sense to consider the finality of things, the *novissimus*. The fullness of humanity is only possible within the scope of the kingdom of Christ, who will, in turn, deliver the kingdom to the Father so that *God may be all in all* (cfr. 1 Cor 15:28). The problem of salvation has to do with the full realization of God's plan in Christ. Because in faith *we know* that this will be fulfilled, *we hope*—for ourselves and for others—to be part of this final joy. This distinction is essential.

In fact, all human beings are subject to God's judgment, and we cannot ever anticipate its outcome[19]. Knowing and hoping are not the same thing. We cannot rest on ourselves or on our possibilities to know; it is Christ in whom we rest. When we look at ourselves we cannot but feel our own fragility. It is precisely because of this that we must take into account, as Karl Rahner reminded us, the possibility of our own perdition before that of others. We cannot deny to any brother or sister the hope that each one of us has placed in our Savior. This hope is offered as the demand of Christian love: «He who accepts the possibility of someone different from himself being forever lost, even if it is only *one*, will have great difficulties to love without reservations ... Even the most tenuous thought of a final hell for others results, in moments when human togetherness is most difficult, in leaving others to themselves»[20]. And to leave others to themselves is something that Christians must never do. We cannot tell God, «Am I my brother's keeper?» (Gen 4:9). «Can Christians speak as assassins? Which human being is not my brother?»[21]. We may also add the early Christian conviction that hell is something neither wanted nor created by God[22].

19 VON BALTHASAR H.U., *Kleiner Diskurs*, 59: «Wir stehen ganz und gar *unter* dem Gericht und haben kein Recht und keine Möglichkeit, dem Richter vorweg in die Karten zu schauen. Wie kann einer Hoffen mit Wissen gleichsetzen?».
20 VERWEYEN J., *Christologische Brennpunkte*, Essen 1977, 119-120. Cited by VON BALTHASAR H.U., *Was dürfen wir hoffen?*, 63; *Kleiner Diskurs*, 59.
21 VON BALTHASAR H.U., *Kleiner Diskurs*, 60.
22 IRENAEUS OF LYONS, *Adv. Haer.* v 27,2: «To those who persevere in his love, he gives his communion. And communion with God is life, light, and fruition of the bounties inherent to him.

The possibility and even the duty of hope for all cannot be confused with the doctrine of *apokatastasis*. The possibility of damnation, above all for oneself, is always before us. *Apokatastasis* is incompatible with the Christian message of salvation, simply because it distorts the message, stripping it of all meaning and significance. It makes automatic what should be the free response of love to the love of God, which offers us, in Christ and in his Spirit, participation in divine life[23]. Maintaining the possibility of eternal damnation is the only guarantee of the truth and reality of the salvation offered to us, which is nothing less than God's love. «Love brings out love,» as Saint Teresa of Avila put it[24]. And love can never be forced; it is necessarily free. God wants there to be some who love with him, and he wants others to have his love in them[25]. If God's life is love, then only in the freedom of love can one be part of his life. Only in love can human fullness exist, and only in freedom can there be a participation in divine love. We cannot doubt God. We should, however, doubt ourselves, according to the Council of Trent (cfr. DH 1534). We know the love of God has no limit, so we can expect that his victory will also know no limit. Thus, we have the possibility of opening ourselves to what the Jesuit theologian Juan Alfaro, in a somewhat different context, called the «certitude of hope»[26].

Whoever on his own, gets away from him, will attain his chosen estrangement. Separation from God is death, as separation from light is darkness: to leave God is the loss of all bounties inherent in him. Those in this predicament who have lost all things with apostasy, devoid of all bounties, live amidst all sorts of pain and grief. It is not that God, on his own looks forward to punishing them, but, in other words, since they are deprived of all bounties, they are haunted by grief and pain».

23 RUIZ DE LA PEÑA J.L., *La pascua de la creación*, Madrid 1996, 237: «Grace, friendship with God, is not imposed by decree; it is freely offered while running the risk of being freely rejected. Hence, in the *real* possibility —which no believer will deny— of a free *yes* to God, there is also the *real* possibility of a *no. Without one, the other would be unsustainable.* Thus, faith has to speak about eternal death as a real possibility. Otherwise, it would undermine the very foundations of the entire economy of salvation. To silence hell, to propose its censorship or systematic veto, allows the irreparable disfiguration of heaven. This entails substituting the God-man dialogue, the outcome of two protagonist freedoms, for the monologue of God, the hegemonic *diktat* of an autocratic and lonely freedom». MARTELET G., *L'au delà retrouvé*, 182: «Jamais Dieu, il est vrai, ne cessera d'aimer, même s'il n'est plus aimé lui-même: mais on pourrait ne pas l'aimer tandis qu'il aime encore et il peut de la sorte arriver qu'il se trouve mis par nous devant *l'envers absolu* de lui-même. En tentant l'impossible afin que son amour soit compris et reçu, il ne peut pas exclure que cet amour, quel immense mystère, devienne cependant un amour rejeté».
24 TERESA OF AVILA, *Libro de la Vida*, 22, 14.
25 DUNS ESCOTO, *Ordinatio* 1. III d. 32, q. unica, n. 6: «[Deus] vult habere alios diligentes, et hoc est velle alios habere amorem suum in se». Cfr. also ibid., III d. 28, q. unica, n. 2, on the perfection of the condilection.
26 ALFARO J., *Esperanza cristiana y liberación del hombre*, Barcelona 1971, 94-96.

Unlike other moments in the history of theology, when the damnation of many was widely accepted, apparently without this conviction creating any problems, today the opposite opinion seems to be sustained by a wide majority. Powerful theological reasons have induced this position. The first and fundamental reason is God's *universal will of salvation*, which knows no limits, and the universality of the salvation that Christ brought us expressed in the paschal mystery, which is source of salvation for all humanity. It has mainly been the eschatological reflection centered in Christology, which was developed during the Second Vatican Council, that has driven Catholic theology toward the positions to which we have referred[27].

3

The Universality of Salvation and Christ's Unique Mediation

A sober analysis of core New Testament texts is, in fact, enough to become aware that passages that deal directly with God's love for the world and his universal will of salvation also speak to Christ's universal mediation; these ideas, which are intrinsically intertwined, are simply two faces of the same coin. We have already cited the fundamental texts of 1 Tim 2:2-7 and John 3:16-17, and we have mentioned numerous other passages that relate to the relevance of Christ's action in terms of the universality that embraces the «whole». All peoples are, without exception, recipients of this message (cfr. Matt 28:19; Mark 16:15-16). The saving action of Christ knows no limits; no one is excluded from it. The difficulty in determining how the effects of this salvation reach everyone should not obstruct the fundamental affirmation of this principle.

In spite of the clarity of these New Testament texts, we find ourselves in a paradoxical situation. The perspective of hope for all finds a broad consensus among our contemporaries, although sometimes in positions that can be lighthearted, as they are prone to deal with human freedom in a trivial manner[28]. Instead, the affirmation of Christ's universal mediation in the salvation that is offered to everyone is sometimes seen as problematic, as we all know. Two New Testament

---

27 Besides the authors cited, cfr., among others, RUIZ DE LA PEÑA J.L., *La pascua de la creación*, 225-226; GARCÍA-MURGA J.R., «¿Dios de amor e infierno eterno?» in *Estudios Eclesiásticos*70 (1995) 3-30.

28 Cfr., for example, SACHS J.S., «Current Eschatology: Universal Salvation and the Problem of Hell» in *Theogical Studies*52 (1991) 227-254.

statements that, as we have seen, appear intimately connected are not always articulated sufficiently. God wants every human being to be saved in Christ and by Christ, and God wants to bring together all things in Christ (Eph 1:10). Everything was created through Christ and for him and has been reconciled through him (cfr. Col 1:16-20; 1 Cor 8:6; Heb 1:2-3; John 1:3-10). In Christ the Father has reconciled the world to himself (cfr. 2 Cor 5:19), and everything is subject to him (Eph 1:22; 1 Cor 15:24-28). The problem that is presented when these two New Testament statements are not seen together is to what extent personal salvation can be seen as participation in Christ's victory. In other words, we face the question of the content and meaning of Christ's mediation: if this mediation is essentially constitutive of salvation, how does the person of Jesus —the way, the truth, and the life— relate to God, toward whom we ultimately move?

The difficulty that has been proposed with urgency in the theology of recent times, with the stimulus being the encounter of the diverse religions and cultures and the dialogue among them, has precedents in ancient times. The Christian belief that Christ is the only path to reach God and salvation is not evident. In fact, pagan common sense was opposed to this, insisting to the contrary that «uno itinere non potest perveniri ad tam grande secretum»[29], that is, one cannot arrive at such a great mystery by means of only one path. Who can say he has the key to access what lies beyond our reach? Would it not be more prudent to speak of complementary paths, of diverse ways to salvation, all of which converge toward this great mystery? We should keep in mind, however, what has already been observed: the saving, universal will of God is intimately linked to the mystery of Christ, and in such a way that, outside the revelation taking place in Christ, we cannot have access to this mystery. We know that God wants the salvation of all humanity because he sent us his Son who died and rose for us. Only in Christ and through Christ do we have access to the knowledge of God's love, of the God who is one and triune, of the God who is our goal and destiny. The revelation of God's saving plan is intimately linked to the revelation of the Trinitarian mystery. The God who wants all humanity to be saved is the Father of

---

29 *Relatio Symmachi praefecti urbis Romae* (To Emperor Valentinian II and to The Roman Senate, in the Year 384), 10 (CSEL 83/3, 27): «Aequum est quicquid omnes colunt unum putari. Eadem spectamus astra, commune caelum est, idem nos mundus involvit; quid interest qua quisque prudentia verum requirat. Uno itinere non potest perveniri ad tam grande secretum». Cfr. RATZINGER J., *Fe, verdad, tolerancia. El cristianismo y las religiones del mundo*, Salamanca, 2005, 66-67.154; GNILKA C., *Chrêsis. Die Methode der Kirchenväter im Umgang mit der antiken Kultur II. Kultur und Conversion*, Basel 1993.

love who sent his Son into the world, so that by the action of the Spirit we may all become his children. Karl Rahner, as is well known, formulated his fundamental axiom of Trinitarian theology, the identity between the economic Trinity and the immanent Trinity, driven by his concern to show that the Trinitarian mystery is the saving mystery *par excellence*[30]. The revelation of this mystery is inseparable from the gift that God makes of himself in his Son and his Holy Spirit. Only in this self-communication is there salvation for humanity, never outside of it. The fullness of revelation is given in Christ because in him the fullness of salvation is given, and vice versa. The Second Vatican Council considered the manifestation that God makes of himself and the decree of his will for the salvation of humanity and the communication of the divine bounties to them to be in intimate unity[31]. In Jesus and the Spirit, God makes us participants in his life, a life that is the eternal exchange of love among the Father, the Son, and the Holy Spirit. In Christ and only in him, the sole mediator between God and humanity, do we have access to this intra-Trinitarian communion. It is only through the Spirit of the Son sent into the world in the fullness of time that we are enabled to cry, «Abba, Father» (cfr. Gal 4:4-6; Rom 8:14-16).

The mystery of God, whom no one has seen (cfr. John 1:18), always transcends us. But, at the same time, the only Son, who is in the Father's bosom, has told us about him (cfr. John 1:18; 14:8). In addressing this difficult balance between the mystery to be safeguarded and the effective and definite revelation that has taken place in Christ, the International Theological Commission pointed out some years ago, in its document *Theology-Christology-Anthropology* (1981), the impossibility of separating the mystery of Christ from the Trinitarian mystery. It denounced the danger of neo-scholastic separation, which did not take sufficiently into account the Trinitarian mystery in order to understand the incarnation or deification of humanity, a danger that in my opinion already has been overcome. Yet at the same time it showed a second danger, a «modern» separation that:

---

[30] Cfr. RAHNER K., «El Dios trino como principio y fundamento trascendente de la historia de la salvación» in *Mysterium Salutis* II/1, Madrid 1969, 360-449, esp. 370-371.

[31] *Dei Verbum* 6: «Through divine revelation, God chose to show forth and communicate himself and the eternal decisions of his will regarding the salvation of humankind. That is to say, he chose to share with them those divine treasures which totally transcend the understanding of the human mind (cfr. Vatican Council I, *Dei Filius*)». *Dei Verbum* 2: «In his goodness and wisdom God chose to reveal himself and to make known to us the hidden purpose of his will (cfr. Eph 1:9) by which through Christ, the Word made flesh, man might in the Holy Spirit have access to the Father and come to share in the divine nature (cfr. Eph 2:18; 2 Pet 1:4)».

places a sort of veil between men and the eternal Trinity, as if Christian revelation did not invite people to the knowledge of the triune God and to share in his life. It leads thus into certain «Agnosticism», which is always unacceptable. Because even though God is always greater than what we can know of him, Christian revelation affirms that the «greater» is always Trinitarian[32].

Even though we are not told in what concrete danger the International Theological Commission was in [because of the agnosticism of not knowing God by any means at all] when it made these affirmations, there is no doubt that, in the years since the document was written, there have been theological propositions that have denied, because of the unknowable nature of the divine mystery, the mediation and universal relevance of Christ regarding the salvation of humanity.

According to these propositions, Jesus would thus be considered merely one among the many mediating figures that have appeared in the course of history. Indeed, according to some who represent this line of thought, it can be difficult, in the face of inter-religious dialogue and the knowledge of the spiritual wealth of other religions, to continue to affirm the superiority of Christianity. Rather, this encounter would make us think that among the great religions there exists an equal measure of good and bad, and that all of them would have practically the same value regarding answers to the transcendent mystery. From the perspective of Christian theology, these theologians intend to found these teachings on Christology and theological doctrines. Given this understanding, that God is unknowable and beyond any established framework, no figure in revelation can make him fully known. On the other hand, there is an insistence on the theocentrism of Jesus, who always related to the Father and before whom he always remained open.

Christian faith in the incarnation does not exclude the idea that the Logos present in Jesus would also be present in other chosen people. In a plurality of mediations, only God's love would remain, making him the only «mediator». These theological propositions hold that the incomprehensibility of God does

---

32 COMISIÓN TEOLÓGICA INTERNACIONAL, *Documentos 1969-1996*, POZO C., S.J. (ed.) BAC, Madrid 1998, I C) 2,1 Madrid 1998, 249. In ibid., I A) i. 2 (p. 246) it said the following: «The separation between Christology and the consideration of the revealed God, within the framework of any period of theology, frequently supposes that the concept of God elaborated by philosophical wisdom is enough in terms of revealed faith. The newness of revelation to the Jewish people as well as the greater radical newness in Christian faith and the value of the event of Jesus Christ are not here foretold. Paradoxically, this separation can reach the conviction that Christological research in itself, is sufficient and can become closed up in itself while dropping any reference to God».

not mean that he has not revealed himself; indeed, quite the contrary should be maintained: God has revealed himself throughout human history, and not just a fragment of it, according to humanity's capacities at the time in question. Since these capacities have varied, revelation has occurred in diverse forms. Thus, it has given origin to different religious experiences, and to explain them, people have used the concepts that, at each moment and in each context, have been available to them. Each of these experiences are valid according to this line of thought, because at the root of all of them is the revelation God has made of himself to humanity. Thus, the Logos has brought about multiple saving manifestations. One of them would be Jesus Christ, decisive for Christians, but does that exclude other religious groups from benefiting from other expressions of God's love and other mediations of salvation?³³. Christ's divinity is even questioned in the most extreme positions in this line of thought, since the presence of the Logos, in the various mediator figures, would be similar to its action among the prophets³⁴.

In response to the theological perspectives described above, it must be said that the universality of revelation, which no doubt has salvation as its intent, is contemplated, in a way, beyond Christ, as if the particular dimension of Christ could impair this universality. We can therefore ask, in terms of Christian revelation and theology, what the idea of universal salvation is all about. That God, somehow, would make himself known to all peoples, beginning with creation

33 Cfr. SCHMIDT-LEUKEL P., «Was will die pluralistitische Religionstheologie?» in *Münchener Theologische Zeitschrift* 49 (1998) 307-334. It is not difficult to discover the influence of ideas from TROELTSCH E., *Die Absolutheit des Christentums und die Religionsgeschichte,* Munich-Hamburg 1969 (first published in 1902). Among the classic writings of recent times on this viewpoint, cfr. HICK J. (ed.), *The Myth of God Incarnate,* London 1977, and especially the article by the same editor: «Jesus and the World Religions», ibid., 172-184. Also from the same author: HICK J., *Problems of Religious Pluralism,* London 1985; and *The Metaphor of God Incarnate,* London 1993. For John Hick, the incarnation would come to be in diverse degrees and modes, and in many diverse persons. Cfr. also KNITTER P.F., *No Other Name? A Critical Survey of Christian Attitudes Toward World Religions,* Maryknoll, New York 1985; and *Jesus and the Other Names. Christian Mission and Global Responsibility,* Maryknoll, New York 1996. Finally: HICK J. - KNITTER P.F. (eds.), *The Myth of Christian Uniqueness: Toward a Pluralistic Theology of Religion,* Maryknoll, New York 1987.

34 *Dominus Iesus* 9 characterizes these viewpoints: «In contemporary theological reflection there often emerges an approach to Jesus of Nazareth that considers him a particular, finite, historical figure, who reveals the divine not in an exclusive way, but in a way complementary with other revelatory and saving figures. The Infinite, the absolute, the ultimate mystery of God would thus manifest itself to humanity in many ways and in many historical figures: Jesus of Nazareth would be one of these. More concretely, for some, Jesus would be one of the many faces which the Logos has assumed in the course of time to communicate with humanity in a saving way». Cfr. also ibid., 4.6.

itself, is evident from a Christian perspective, but, at the same time, it is also evident that this creation moves toward Christ. Thus, there occurs with equal clarity a particular event, which in its unforeseen newness gives meaning and is the fulfillment of all other forms of God's manifestation to humanity. To the impossibility of knowing God is necessarily added the impossibility of understanding the salvation that is offered to us, and these two aspects condition one another. In the New Testament, the contents of salvation are clearly related to and linked with Jesus —the importance of conforming oneself with Christ, entering the divine Sonship created in his image, rising with him, and so forth. The salvation brought to us by Christ is only understood as a participation in the perfection that Christ himself attained in his humanity upon being raised and glorified by God the Father. What Jesus gains for himself as head of the body is destined for all humanity. Athanasius of Alexandria spoke in these terms:

> Everything Scripture says that Jesus has received, it says so because of his body, which is first fruit of the Church… In the first place the Lord has raised his own body and has exalted it. Then he has raised all its members to give them, as God, what he has received as Man[35].

What Jesus attained for himself as head of the body is destined for all peoples. The affirmations on the unique mediation of Jesus and the universality of salvation are harmonized in these passages, as well as others that could be mentioned here, which insist on the incorporation of all humanity into Christ by virtue of the incarnation[36]. Let us focus on one, a text from the Quiercy Synod in the year 853, which summarizes in a few words the essential contents of New Testament and early patristic theology:

---

[35] *De Incarnatione Verbi et contra Arianos* 12 (PG 26,1004). *Contra Arianos* I 47 (PG 26,109): «It is not the Logos, as Logos and Wisdom, who is anointed with the Holy Spirit given by him, but it is the flesh he has assumed which is anointed in him and for him, so that the holiness that has come upon the Lord as man may reach all humans from him». Ibid., I 48 (PG 26,113): «He sanctifies himself (cfr. John 17:10), so that we be sanctified in him». Cfr. LADARIA L.F., «Atanasio de Alejandría y la unción de Cristo (*Contra Arianos* I 47-50)» in GUIJARRO S. - FERNÁNDEZ SANGRADOR F. (eds.), *Plenitudo temporis: Homenaje al Prof. Dr. Ramón Trevijano Etcheverría*, Pontificia Universidad de Salamanca, Salamanca 2002, 469-479. More generally, LADARIA L.F., «Salvezza di Cristo e salvezza dell'uomo» in *Archivio Teologico Torinese* 11 (2005) 35-52 (cfr. Ch.3 of this book).

[36] We are satisfied with a few references: IRENAEUS OF LYONS, *Adv. Haer.* III 19,3 (SCh 211,282); V 36,3 (ORBE A., *Teología de San Ireneo III*, Madrid-Toledo 1988, 632-665); HILARY OF POITIERS, *In Matt.* 4:12 (SCh 254,130); 18,6 (SCh 258,80); *Trin.* II 24 (CCL 62,60); *Tr. Ps.* 51,16-17 (CCL 61,104); 54,9 (146);

As there is not, there was not, nor will there be any human being whose nature was not assumed by him; likewise, there is not, there was not, nor will there be any human being for whom Christ Jesus our Lord will not have suffered even though not everyone will be redeemed by the mystery of his passion. Now, that not all are redeemed by the mystery of his passion does not reflect on the magnitude and volume of the price, but on the part of the infidels and of those who do not believe with that faith that «works through love» (Gal 5:6; DH 624; cfr. also DH 623).

Catholic theology and the teachings of the Church regarding the question of «infidels» is resolved here in an expeditious manner. But let us stay with the main affirmations. There is not —nor will there be— any human being whose nature has not been assumed by Christ Jesus; the Second Vatican Council formulates that the Son of God, through his incarnation, has become united, in a certain way *(quodammodo)*, with all humanity (GS 22). Both texts gather a rich tradition that is the foundation of the universality of Christian soteriology[37]. There is no contradiction between universality and unity. The head and the body form the one and only Christ. Jesus cannot be thought of independently from his Church and the whole of humanity, in which the Church is intentionally included.

Against the law of logic proposing the universal to be abstract and the concrete to be only particular, both terms can be applied to Christ, because Christ is neither a general law nor an abstract idea, nor simply a particular individual. As the Word made flesh in history he bears in himself the universality of God and the universality of humanity; it is his reality. The life of Jesus in its concrete particularity comprising death and resurrection is the expression of the totality of God for the world and the totality of man for God … God is not an individual among others; it is what happens in Christ. As man-God he is equally unique; he is not a human element who can be generalized. The humanity of Jesus assumes in His concrete originality «the universally human»[38].

GREGORY OF NYSSA, *Contra Apollinarem* I 16 (PG 45,1153); CYRIL OF ALEXANDRIA, *In Johannis Evangelium* I 9 (PG 73,161-164). On the other hand, one cannot forget the personal responsibility of each human being in accepting or rejecting their free decision to become incorporated into Christ, and to remain united with him as the vine's root is to the vine, or to reject this communion; cfr. HILARY OF POITIERS, *Tr. Ps.* 52,16-17 (CCL 61,104). Therefore, we will not find ourselves automatically saved due to the fact of all having been included in Christ.

37 GONZÁLEZ DE CARDEDAL O., *Cristología*, BAC, Madrid 2005, 528: «The inclusion of all of humanity in Christ (creation, incarnation, redemption) is the premise of all the New Testament statements about our redemption».

38 SEBOÜÉ B., *Jesucristo, el único mediador. Ensayo sobre la redención y la salvación. Tomo I*, Sígueme, Salamanca, 402. The author did not modify his thinking in the second edition of his work, *Jésus-*

From a different perspective, to what objective do the complementary paths of revelation and knowledge of God lead? From the point of view of those who hold the differing theological perspective discussed earlier, it is possible to conceive of diverse contents of salvation according to the different religions or paths through which each one has come to it[39]. Immediately, the difficulties facing this proposition are obvious. Could we still speak of the unity of the human race if there were different final vocations for humanity? This question, at least, does not seem to lack meaning. The very reasons for the universality of salvation that were indicated, as we have seen, by the Second Vatican Council would be placed in doubt. The unity of humanity's origin and destiny must be seen as intimately related. Only thus can we affirm the existence of an intrinsic relationship between protology and eschatology. Does every human being have some relationship to Christ by the mere fact of his coming into the world? There are many reasons that affirm this. According to the Second Vatican Council, Christ is not only «perfectly man», but also «the perfect man», and in him the mystery of humanity acquires its definitive light (cfr. GS 22;41)[40]. In Christ, God gives us his bounty, beginning with the gifts of creation, and we have no information of other paths through which his bounty may reach us: «He who did not withhold his own Son, but gave him up for all of us, will he not with him also give us everything else?» (Rom 8:32). Only through Christ and in Christ does God give us all things, because in him we have been chosen before the creation of the world, and everything must have him as its head (cfr. Eph 1:3-10). If the gift of the Son —once for all time— appears problematic, what bounty can we expect from God? His infinite bounty embracing all of humanity is known to us through Christ's revelation. In him, God's love for all peoples has been made known. Does it make sense to speak of God's love outside of Christ or without relating to him?

    Christ, l'unique médiateur. Essai sur la rédemption et le salut, Paris 2003, 275. On the question of the *universale concretum,* cfr. PIÉ-NINOT S., «Unicidad y universalidad salvífica de Jesucristo como *universale concretum personale*» published in *Antropología y fe cristiana.* IV *Jornadas de Teología,* Santiago de Compostela 2003, 279-305.

39 Cfr, for example, HEIM S.M., «Salvation. A More Pluralistic Hypothesis» in *Modern Theology* 10 (1994) 341-360.

40 The Council left open, at least in some measure, the precise scope of these affirmations. Post-Conciliar theological developments have underscored the Christological relevance of protology and, in fact, anthropology. To cite a few examples, cfr. RAHNER K., *Grundkurs des Glaubens,* Freiburg 1976, 211-226; VON BALTHASAR H.U., *Theologie II: Wahrheit Gottes,* Einsiedeln 1985, 73.76. On this body of problems, cfr. LADARIA L.F., «Cristo "perfecto hombre" y "hombre perfecto"» in BENAVENT E. - VIDAL M. - MORALI I. (eds), *Sentire cum Ecclesia. Homenaje al P. Karl Josef Becker* SJ, Facultad de Teología San Vicente Ferrer, Valencia 2003, 171-185.

Is God's love for humanity even possible without it being linked to the love that the Father has for the Son, his «beloved,» the «favored one» *par excellence* (cfr. Mark 1:11; 9:7; Col 1:13; John 15:9; 17:23, 26)? Who is ultimately the God who can be reached through so many equivalent and complementary paths? It is the God who is always greater and more mysterious, one and triune, the Father who sent his incarnate Son into the world and the Spirit of his Son into our hearts so that we may live as children of God (cfr. Gal 4:4-6).

Other authors, in a more nuanced fashion, have tried to provide a rationale for the saving meaning found in other religions and the universality of salvation by making a distinction between the particular historical event of Christ and the universal action of the divine Logos «as such». The incarnation was a unique and unrepeatable event. In Jesus we have the greatest and fullest manifestation of God, but the historic particularity of Christ imposes certain limitations on the significance of the Son of God coming into the world. It cannot be an absolute occurrence, as no historic singularity may be considered as such. God is absolute, but no religion can be. If, on the one hand, the Logos took shape in a unique way at the incarnation, then on the other hand all of creation is filled with the divine Logos. Because of this, the economy of the incarnate Word may be considered to be the «sacrament» of a broader economy, that of the eternal Word of God, which coincides with the religious history of humanity. Christianity does not exclude other modes of God's presence in human history; otherwise, the historic particularity of Jesus would be confused with the fullness of the invisible God[41].

Although the fullness of the revelation of the triune God in Jesus Christ and his oneness are not directly in question, these positions and other similar ones provoke doubt regarding the acceptance of the reality of the Son's incarnation, as he, from the moment he became man, existed only in the humanity he assumed, according to hypostasis. In practice, a greater universal validity is assigned to the saving action of the eternal Word than to the incarnate Word. But the universal mediation spoken of in the New Testament and in the tradition of the Church clearly refers to Jesus Christ, the Son of God made man. «With the incarnation,

---

41 Cfr. among other examples, SCHILLEBEECKX E., *Umanità. Storia di Dio*, Brescia 1992, 219-220; GEFFRÉ C., «La singolarità del cristianesimo nell'età del pluralismo religioso» in *Filosofia e Teologia* 6 (1992) 38-52; «La verité du christianisme a l'âge du pluralisme religieux» in *Angelicum* 74 (1997) 177-191; «Pour un christianisme mondial» in *Recherches de Science Religieuse* 86 (1998) 53-75; DUPUIS J., *Hacia una teología cristiana del pluralismo religioso*, Sal Terrae, Santander 2000; «Le Verbe de Dieu, Jésus-Christ et les religions du monde» in *Nouvelle Revue Theologique* 123 (2001) 229-246.

all the saving actions of the Word of God are always done in unity with the human nature that he has assumed for the salvation of all people»[42].

There is no Logos other than the incarnate one. What corresponds to his divinity also corresponds to his humanity. But the two natures are not confused with one another. In keeping with the well-known formula of Saint Leo the Great, each acts in accordance to what is proper to itself in communion with the other (cfr. DH 294). Given that in the Lord Jesus the divine person and the human person are one, both the shame and the glory are common to his divinity and his humanity, although each of the two natures present in Jesus do not derive from the same principle (cfr. DH 295). So an action of the Word in its divine nature lacking communion with the human nature must be excluded. The one and only subject is at the same time inseparably divine and human. If there is no possibility for the Logos not to be united with the flesh, then divine actions cannot be carried out without the humanity, and vice versa (cfr. DH 317-318). This is the consequence of the seriousness of the incarnation: that the only divine person of the Son became at the incarnation, considering that he subsists in two natures, a «persona composite», according to Thomas Aquinas[43]. Even before these dogmatic formulations became precise, Saint Irenaeus said the following:

> [Gnostics] being ignorant that his [God's] only-begotten Word, who is always present with the human race, united to and mingled with His own creation, according to the Father's pleasure, and who became flesh, is himself Jesus Christ our Lord, who did also suffer for us, and rose again on our behalf, and who will come again in the glory of his Father, to raise up all flesh … There is … one God the Father, and one Christ Jesus, who came by means of the whole dispensational arrangements [connected to him], and gathered together all things in Himself[44].

There seems to be no room for any aspect or dimension of the Son that was not «affected» by his incarnation and the paschal mystery of his death and resurrection.

---

42 *Dominus Iesus* 10. The text states the following: «The one subject which operates in the two natures, human and divine, is the single person of the Word. Therefore, the theory which would attribute, after the incarnation as well, a saving activity to the Logos as such in his divinity, exercised "in addition to" or "beyond" the humanity of Christ, is not compatible with the Catholic faith».

43 THOMAS AQUINAS, *STh* III 2,4: «Et sic dicitur persona composita in quantum unum duobus subsistit». Cfr. JOHN OF DAMASCUS, *De fide ortodoxa* III 4 (PG 94,997).

44 IRENAEUS OF LYONS, *Adv. Haer.* III 16,6 (SCh 211,312-314). Cfr. also LADARIA L.F., «Il Logos incarnato e lo Spirito Santo nell'opera della salvezza» in *Congregazione per la Dottrina della Fede: Dichiarazione* «Dominus Iesu» *Documenti e studi*. Città del Vaticano 2002, 85-97.

The incarnate, dead, and resurrected one brings together in himself all things because he has made himself present throughout the whole economy. The unity of this economy seems compromised if we think of saving actions that, after the incarnation and Easter, do not stem from the incarnate Son, divine and human, dead and risen. The meaning of Jesus Christ for the human race and its history is absolutely singular and unique[45]. It is paradoxical that the salvation offered to all humanity and Christ's universal mediation have been perceived as oppositional and not in mutual relationship. Perhaps this has been influenced by the diverse interpretations of the axiom *extra Ecclesiam nulla salus* and its conflicting history. Christ's mediation has perhaps been linked to a strict, unsustainable interpretation of this principle. Salvation outside the Church, or at least its visible frontiers, would mean salvation outside of Christ[46]. It seems evident that this deduction is not correct. In the intimate association of the mystery of Christ and his Church, distinctions are important[47]. The Church is, above all, saved and not saving, and it is solely by the virtue of Christ and his Spirit that the Church exercises a function in the divine plan—a function that, as a sign and instrument (sacrament) of the union of all humanity with God, prevents us from seeing the Church as an obstacle to those who have not been incorporated into it.

In Christ and only in him do we have salvation and the redemption of our sins. He redeemed all of humanity, and this saving function remains exclusively his. Hilary of Poitiers made a theologically suggestive comment on the Gospel scene in Matt 14:28-31 where Peter wants to go to Jesus over the water and sinks;

---

45 *Dominus Iesus* 15: «From the beginning, the community of believers has recognized in Jesus a salvific value such that he alone, as Son of God made man, crucified and risen, by the mission received from the Father and in the power of the Holy Spirit, bestows revelation (cfr. Matt 11:27) and divine life (cfr. John 1:12; 5:25-26; 17:2) to all humanity and to every person. In this sense, one can and must say that Jesus Christ has a significance and a value for the human race and its history, which are unique and singular, proper to him alone, exclusive, universal, and absolute. Jesus is, in fact, the Word of God made man for the salvation of all».

46 Cfr. the recent book of SESBOÜÉ B., *Hors de l'Église pas de salut. Histoire d'une formule et problèmes d'interprétation*, Paris 2004; DE LUBAC H., *Catholicisme. Les aspects sociaux du dogme*, Paris 1983, 179-205.

47 *Dominus Iesus* 16: «As the head and members of a living body, though not identical, are inseparable, so too Christ and the Church can neither be confused nor separated, and constitute a single "whole Christ"». We cannot now deal with the complexity of problems of the function of the Church in the salvation of those who do not belong to it. Cfr. JOHN PAUL II, *Redemptoris Missio* 9-10. The Church, the universal sacrament of salvation, is necessary for salvation. The salvation of Christ is received by non-Christians by virtue of a grace that has a mysterious relationship with the Church, although it may not formally introduce them to it.

the Lord has to give him a hand to climb into the boat. Poitiers claimed that this story offers a *typical* interpretation. Everyone, Peter included, had to be saved by Jesus; he is the only one who dies for everyone. In his redemptive passion, he could not have any companion, precisely because there cannot be any companion in something that only one does for all[48]. No one can add anything to the sole mediator's offering, because, as the firstborn of the Father, no one else can compare with him. Only though him, by virtue of his unique condition, could salvation come to humanity, his brothers and sisters. The fathers of the fourth century repeatedly argued that Arians, by ignoring the divinity of Jesus, denied the salvation of all humanity[49], to whom Jesus united himself at his incarnation, so as to be able to communicate to us the bounty of the divine life. But this unity and universality of Christ, in whom salvation was offered and fulfilled, once for all time, as well as God's universal will of salvation, should not be interpreted, in the words of Hans Urs von Balthasar, in *exclusive* terms, but rather in *inclusive* ones. In other words, Christ is the sole mediator, inasmuch as his presence is universal and unlimited.

The ancient theology of the seed of the Word is a sufficiently eloquent expression to highlight the universality of his presence. On the one hand, it is clearly established that the totality of the Logos is in Christ, but this does not prevent us from affirming his universal presence as well. Citing a few texts will suffice to demonstrate this. Justin, the philosopher and martyr, said: «We have been taught that Christ is the first-born of God, and we have declared above that he is the Word of whom every race of men were partakers; and those who lived reasonably are Christians, even though they have been thought atheists»[50]. He added:

---

48 HILARY OF POITIERS, *In Matt* 14:16 (SCh 258,30): «Indeed Peter was not unworthy of approaching the Lord, and in fact he tried to do so, but in this fact it is observed as a typical interpretation *(typicus ordo)*. As the Lord, who stepped into riots and storms of this world, he could not make anyone else participant of his passion. He alone was to suffer for all and was to redeem the sins of all and does not allow any fellow sufferer for what is given to all by only One *(solus enim passurus pro omnibus omnium peccata soluebat, nec sociom admittit quicquid universitati praestatur ab uno)*. Him being the redemption of all, so also Peter had to be redeemed, as he was reserved to be the guarantee of this redemption as martyr of Christ». The term *universitas*, very much Hilary's, frequently refers to the totality of humanity inasmuch as it is united and included in Christ. Cfr. PETORELLI J.P., «Le thème de Sion expression de la théologie de la rédemption dans l'oeuvre de saint Hilaire de Poitiers» in *Hilaire et son temps. Actes du Colloque de Poitiers* (29 September- October 3 1968), Paris 1969, 213-233. AMBROSE OF MILAN, *In Ps.* 118 8,57 (*Opera* 9,370): «Mysticus autem ille sol iustitiae omnibus ortus est, omnibus venit, omnibus passus est et omnibus resurrexit».

49 HILARY OF POITIERS, *Trin.* XII 36 (CCL 62A,606); AMBROSE OF MILAN, *De Fide* IV 10,130 (*Opera* 15,316).

50 JUSTIN, *Apologia* I 46,2-3 (Wartelle, 160). I've taken the translation into Spanish done by RUIZ BUENO D., *Padres Apologetas Griegos* (BAC 116, 232).

«And there is nothing wonderful about it; if the demons are proved to cause those to be hated even more who do not live according to only a part of the word poured out on humanity but according to the knowledge and contemplation of the whole Word, which is Christ»[51].

There is no contradiction, therefore, between the total presence of the Word in Christ, the fullness of the revelation, and his universal presence, which is less full, partial, and participating in, but not lacking in meaning for the salvation of all humanity. Not only is there no contradiction, but one mutually requires the other. This is the case because the universal presence makes sense as a radiation of the fullness of the Word in person, the Son of God made flesh. And, at the same time, this total presence carries in itself the dynamism of universality: it would not be full if it did not have meaning for all humanity. Not far from this fundamental concern, which was already present in early Christianity, is the recently developed doctrine concerning participating mediations, which, in the context of the sole mediation of Christ and without being parallel or complementary to it, can gain meaning and value by receiving their power from Jesus, the sole savior[52]. Jesus includes everyone and excludes no one, and all of us have received his fullness (cfr. John 1:16). The universality of salvation and the unity of Christ's mediation mutually affirm each other. They are not two incompatible facts; rather, they illuminate and require the other.

51 JUSTIN, *Apologia* II 8,3 (Wartelle, 208). Cfr. RUIZ BUENO D., op. cit.., 269. Cfr. also CLEMENT OF ALEXANDRIA, *Protr.* I 5,4; X 98,4 (SCh 2bis,60; 166). Cfr. COMISIÓN TEOLÓGICA INTERNACIONAL, *El cristianismo y las otras* religiones, 41-45. *Documentos 1969-1996*, POZO C., S.J. (ed.) BAC, Madrid 1998, 572-573.
52 It seems especially significant that the Declaration *Dominus Iesus* 14, when inviting today's theology to explore if and in what measure positive figures and elements of other religions can enter into the divine plan of salvation, it mentions *Lumen Gentium* 62, on the multiple cooperation of creatures elicited by the unique mediation of the Redeemer (the immediate context deals with the function of Mary), and another of *Redemptoris Missio* 5, on participated mediations of a diverse order in the broader context of spiritual richness and the bounty that God has given to all peoples and cultures.

4
The Universality of the Gift of the Spirit

A reflection on the universality of salvation cannot be made without referring to pneumatology. «I will pour out my Spirit upon all flesh», proclaims the prophecy of Joel, which, on Pentecost, Peter deemed to be already fulfilled (cfr. Acts 2:14-21; Joel 3:1-5). «The Spirit of the Lord has filled the world» (Wis 1:7). By definition, the Spirit has no limitations, nor can he be controlled. He resists any localizing. It is not difficult from this point of view to relate the universality of salvation to the Holy Spirit. More difficulties can be created by the link between the universality of Christ and that of the Spirit. But, in fact, from the premise that the Spirit cannot be limited in his faculty of inspiration (cfr. John 3:8), the saving presence of the divine Spirit has been proposed to be greater and more universal than that of Christ, who, in his humanity, necessarily limited the universality of the Spirit. Christ's saving action would be only one of the manifestations of the universal performance of the Spirit, perhaps the fullest and most radical, but he would not be able to vindicate its exclusivity[53]. But can there be, according to the New Testament, a universality of the action of the Spirit not linked to that of Jesus? Can the presence of the Spirit be more universal and broader than the presence of Christ, who was born, died, rose, and «ascended far above all the heavens, so that he might fill all things» (Eph 4:10)?

The New Testament speaks of Jesus' gift of the Spirit, but not without speaking of the Spirit's presence in Jesus himself. According to Basil the Great, «the things done in the dispensation of the coming of our Lord in the flesh ...every operation was wrought with the co-operation of the Spirit»[54]. The Holy Spirit took part in the incarnation of Jesus (cfr. Matt 1:18-20; Luke 1: 35), descended upon him during his baptism, and anointed him at the Jordan (cfr. Mark 1:9-11; Luke 4:18; Acts 10:38). From this moment, the Spirit stayed with him and rested

---

53 *Dominus Iesus* 12: «There are also those who propose the hypothesis of an economy of the Holy Spirit with a more universal breadth than that of the incarnate Word, crucified and risen. This position also is contrary to the Catholic faith, which, on the contrary, considers the salvific incarnation of the Word as a trinitarian event. In the New Testament, the mystery of Jesus, the incarnate Word, constitutes the place of the Holy Spirit's presence as well as the principle of the Spirit's outpouring on humanity, not only in messianic times (cfr. Acts 2:32-36; John 7:39; 20:22; 1 Cor 15:45), but also prior to his coming in history (cfr. 1 Cor 10:4; 1 Pet 1:10-12)».

54 BASIL THE GREAT, *De Spiritu sancto* 16,39 (SCh 17 bis, 386).

upon him (cfr. John 1:32-34). Jesus offered himself to the Father at the moment of his passion by virtue of the eternal Spirit (cfr. Heb 9:24)[55] and was constituted as the Son of God according to the Spirit of holiness by his resurrection from the dead (cfr. Rom 1:4). The door to the gift of the Spirit is opened by the glorification of the Lord at his resurrection (cfr. John 7:39). Jesus, risen and exalted, receives the outpouring of the Spirit from the Father so that he shares it with humanity (cfr. Acts 2:33). The Spirit is communicated to us as a gift of the risen Jesus Christ (cfr. John 20:22), which is why he is called the Spirit of Christ, of Jesus, and of Jesus Christ (cfr. Rom 8:9; 1 Pet 1:1; Acts 16:7; Phil 1:19; Gal 4:6). The Lord gives us the Spirit because his very humanity is thoroughly penetrated by him and transformed into «life-giving spirit» (1 Cor 15:45). Patristic theology saw an essential relationship between the «newness» of the Lord in the resurrection and the newness of the gift of the Spirit. Thus, the Spirit, according to Saint Irenaeus, renews all human beings «from their old habits into the newness of Christ beginning with the old age into the newness of Christ»[56]. And Origen added the following:

> Our Savior also, after the resurrection, when old things had already passed away, and all things had become new, himself a new man, and the first-born from the dead (cfr. Col 1:18), his apostles also being renewed by faith in his resurrection, says, «Receive the Holy Spirit» (John 20:22). This is doubtless what the Lord the Savior meant to convey in the Gospel (cfr. Matt 9:17), when he said that new wine cannot be put into old wineskins, but commanded that the wineskins should be made new, i.e., that men should walk in newness of life (cfr. Rom 6:4), that they might receive the new wine, i.e., the newness of grace of the Holy Spirit[57].

The newness of life —of Jesus and of humanity— is the work of the Spirit of Jesus. In the Spirit of the Son, we can call God Father (cfr. Gal 4:6; Rom 8:15). The salvation that the Spirit brings us is our conformity with Christ, divine Sonship, and resurrection with him (cfr. Rom 8:11). The New Testament and the tradition of the Church have essentially linked the gift of the Spirit to the risen Lord;

---

55 Cfr. VANHOYE A., «L'Esprit éternel et le feu du sacrifice» in *Biblica* 64 (1983) 263-274.
56 IRENAEUS OF LYONS, *Adv. Haer.* III 17,1 (SCh 211,330).
57 ORIGEN, *De principiis* I 3,7 (SCh 252,158); cfr. also ibid., II 7,2 (328).

Neither the New Testament nor the tradition of the Church knows of a gift of the the outpouring of the Spirit has its origins in the glorified humanity of Jesus[58]. Spirit that is not somehow linked to the resurrection of Jesus and not oriented to the consummation of his saving work. Jesus' humanity is the place of the presence of the Holy Spirit in the world, and this humanity, once glorified in the resurrection and exalted, is the beginning of the outpouring of the Spirit upon all of humanity[59]. The Holy Spirit has his natural place in the Church, the body of Christ[60], but that is not an obstacle for his universal presence, as salvation in Christ is extended to everyone[61]. In the Spirit, through Christ, we have access to the Father (cfr. Eph 2:18), who is, as we have seen, the goal and ultimate destiny of every human being. The unity of our origin, and above all, the unity of our destiny guarantee the ultimate unity of the human species, who has in Christ its center and point of convergence (cfr. *Gaudium et Spes* 10;45). The universality of the Spirit cannot be separated from the universality of Christ, from the universal lordship and dominion over all that he gained through his resurrection. Moreover, the universal presence of the Spirit attests to the fact that the risen Lord is present everywhere. Hilary of Poitiers voiced this view in his commentary on Psalm 57 (56):

The prophet announces with his wish that God should be exalted over the heavens (cfr. Ps 57:6). And because after having been exalted over the heavens he had to fill everything with the glory of his Holy Spirit [the psalmist] adds: «Let your glory be over all earth» (Ps 57:5). Because the gift of the Spirit shed over all flesh was going to be testimony of the glory of the Lord exalted over the heavens[62].

---

58 IRENAEUS OF LYONS, *Adv. Haer.* III 24,1 (SCh 211,472): «deposita est [in Ecclesia] communicatio Christi, id est Spiritus Sanctus»; ATHANASIUS OF ALEXANDRIA, *Ad. Serap.* I 23 (PG 26,565): «The stamp carries the shape of Christ who is the one that stamps, of whom become participants those that are stamped»; BASIL OF CAESAREA, *De Spiritu Sancto* 18,46 (SCh 17 bis,410): «[The Holy Spirit] as Paraclete carries the trace of the bounty of the Paraclete who has sent him».

59 Cfr. *Dominus Iesus* 12.

60 IRENAEUS OF LYONS, *Adv. Haer.* III 24,1 (SCh 211,474): «Where the Spirit of the Lord is, there is the Church, and where the Church is, there is the Spirit of the Lord and all grace».

61 Cfr. JOHN PAUL II, *Redemptoris Missio*, 28-29.

62 HILARY OF POITIERS, *Tr. Ps.* 56,6 (CCL 61,164).

The universality of Christ and the universality of the Spirit go together and cannot be understood without the other. Without the Spirit, the work of the Savior is not fulfilled in us. The universal relevance of Christ and of the Spirit is necessary for the universality of salvation. It cannot be otherwise if, according to Christian conviction, it is only through Jesus that the Spirit may come upon those who believe in him and upon all of humanity[63]. Without both the incarnate Son and the Spirit, the saving plan of the Father, which embraces all of humanity, is not realized. There is only one economy of salvation, which began with Christ's being chosen before the creation of the world and ends with the bringing of all things together in Christ (cfr. Eph 3:1-10). The Father executes this design through Jesus and in the power of the Spirit, who, in union with him, has been pouring his grace upon us since the resurrection.

5

The Symphony of Salvation

We have already mentioned in this presentation a fundamental passage of *Gaudium et Spes* 22, with which we will now conclude, although we will dispense with citing it again. This passage gives us an excellent synthesis of the dynamics of universal salvation, which has its realization and foundation in the paschal mystery. The universality of Christ's work is centered in the fact that he died on behalf of us all. Yet by dying, he gave us life, that is, the life of his resurrection. Even those who do not know him are called to this divine vocation, that is, to the perfect *sonship* in and through Christ. Christians and non-Christians reach this goal by virtue of the gift of the Spirit that associates us with the unique paschal

---

63 JUSTIN, *Dial. Tryph.* 87,5-6 (PTS 47,222): «Hence, they rested, that is, they ceased, the gifts of the Spirit, once he who had to come arrived, after whom… they had to cease in you and resting upon him, to become again gifts Christ delivers to those who believe in him… I already told you as it was foretold what he was to do after his ascension into the heavens, and now I repeat it to you. Scriptures then said: When he ascended "on high, he made captivity itself a captive. He gave gifts to his people" (Ps 67:18; Eph 4:8). And again it is said in another prophecy: "In the last days it will be, God declares, that I will pour out my Spirit upon all flesh… even upon my slaves, both men and women, in those days I will pour out my spirit; and they will prophesy"» (Joel 3:1-2; Acts 2:17-18). There is no need to underscore that the fullness of the *pneuma* in Christ is related to his condition as the personal Logos, which was already possessed by the Spirit from the moment he was anointed by the Father in the power of the divine Spirit to be able to attest to creation, and that was received in a new outpouring after the incarnation to carry out the salvific work and to communicate the Spirit to his human brothers and sisters.

mystery of Christ, even if it is through diverse paths known only to God[64]. Saint Irenaeus spoke of the «symphony of salvation», referring to the diverse ways through which, in the time of the Old Testament, the Father, rich and great, guided humanity toward salvation through the Word and the many gifts of the Spirit[65]. Everyone has access to this ultimate goal, which is God the Father, through the Son, who became incarnate for us, and in the Spirit of Jesus. This unique path is open to us all: «Patet ergo universis per coniunctionem carnis aditus in Christo»[66].

---

[64] Cfr. a similar expression in *Ad Gentes* 7.

[65] IRENAEUS OF LYONS, *Adv. Haer.* IV 14,2 (SCh 100,544-46): «He needed no one; rather he gave his communion to those who needed him. And to those who pleased him he drew them as architect the building of the saving ark. And those who in Egypt were blind he became their personal guide. And those roaming restless in the desert he gave them a most comfortable law. And those who entered into the good land he gave them a worthy inheritance. And those who return [in repentance] to the Father, he offers the fatted calf and he gives the best garment (cfr. Luke 15:22ff.). Of many modes the human lineage arranged for the symphony of salvation (cfr. Luke 15:25). Thus, John says in the Apocalypse (1:15): "And his voice was like the sound of many waters". Many waters are, indeed, truly the Spirit, by how rich and great is the Father. And through all of them he validated the Word, devoid of any discontent, for all under his reign; drawing for all creatures a convenient and appropriate law». Cfr. also LEO THE GREAT, *In nat. Domini* 4,1 (PL 54,203): «Sacramentum salutis humanae nulla umquam antiquitate cessavit... Semper quidem, dilectissimi, diversis modis multisque mensuris humano generi bonitas divina consuluit. Et plurima providentiae suae munera omnibus retro saeculis clementer impertuit».

[66] HILARY OF POITIERS, *Tr. Ps.* 91,9 (CCL 61,329).

Jesus Christ Salvation of All

This book was printed on *thin opaque smooth white Bible paper*, using the *Minion* and *Type Embellishments One* font families.

This edition was printed in D'VINNI, S.A., in Bogotá, Colombia, during the last weeks of the ninth month of year two thousand eight.

Ad publicam lucem datus mense septembre in nativitate Sancte Marie